AF490202

PRAISE FOR *WOMEN WIRED TO WIN*

"I laughed. I cried. I underlined half the book. With grit, grace, and the wisdom of someone who's walked through fire, Susan Norman shows what's possible when faith meets fierce determination. She may just be the Zig Ziglar of a new generation of women entrepreneurs—bold, faith-fueled, and fiercely real.

Susan doesn't just teach success; she embodies it, turning adversity into authority and pain into purpose. Her story will ignite something deep in every woman who's ever dared to dream, fought to rise, and refused to settle.

This isn't just for direct sellers—it's for any woman ready to rise into her God-given destiny. *Women Wired to Win* dares you to chase the dream in your heart and equips you with the tools to actually do it. Susan Norman writes like a coach and a sister in the trenches. You'll finish this book braver, bolder, and ready to build the life God designed for you."

—**Susan L. Davis**,
author of *63 Hours in Hell*

"*Women Wired to Win* came to me at the exact moment I needed it! Becoming an entrepreneur is not for the faint of heart, and you need all the words of faith and encouragement that this book provides.

Susan's ability to draw the reader in and relate to them as if she were a friend sitting across from you over coffee giving you stellar advice is what makes this book so special.

She has been there—you see it, you feel it, you know it—and she is sharing all the tools in her toolkit to make sure you benefit from her experiences, the good, the bad, and the ugly. A must-read for anyone starting or restarting a business in the social marketing space!"

—**Jennifer Desrochers**, RN, MS, BC-FHNC,
Founder/Owner of JLD Wellness, LLC

"If you are feeling called toward a greater purpose—one that has a positive impact on the lives of others and honors the gifts God has given you—this book will speak to your heart. Susan writes with both encouragement and honesty by sharing the real struggles behind her journey and how her determination, resilience, and faith shaped her success. With practical, applicable steps, she offers a clear roadmap and dares us to take our own dreams from mere wishes to reality!"

—**Kim Logan**,
grammygoinggreen.com

"*Women Wired to Win* will help many direct sales leaders shift the way they lead in life and business. I enjoyed how Susan wove her triumphs and trials throughout a blueprint for women who are ready to play big in every area of their lives. With a commitment to bridge the gap between faith and finance, Susan has written a book that will be a defining moment for women who are truly ready to win."

—**Dr. Darnyelle Jervey-Harmon**,
bestselling author of *Move to Millions:
The Proven Framework to Become a Million Dollar
CEO with Grace & Ease Instead of Hustle & Grind*

"Susan has created a simple step-by-step guide to success. Every direct seller should get this book at the very start of their journey—I believe it will make all the difference!"

—**Lisa Taylor**, Style By Lisa,
Independent Beauty Consultant

"Susan's book came along at the perfect time in my life. With nearly 20 years of experience in the HR world, and tons of life experience including a significant life shift in 2020, I've been focused on pivoting my consulting business. When I read Susan's book, not only did she provide an excellent roadmap of experience, but I also felt seen. She's been there, and she understands what it takes to be successful. Her book is so inspiring and encouraging! I felt like I was talking to a trusted friend."

—**Heather Brayshaw**, SHRM-CP, SPHR,
founder of HR Heather

"What stood out most to me was how Susan made Christ the center of *Women Wired to Win*. This book shows faith and perseverance while sharing the love of Jesus. It's a roadmap that anyone can understand, filled with personal experiences of going from rock bottom to redemption. It's easily understood and practical, with real application that anyone can follow. I'm recommending it to my entire Mary Kay team—it's exactly what every entrepreneur needs."

—**Gwen C. Hardy**, Senior Vice President,
Members First Credit Union

"WOW! Just wow. I just finished reading this book and I have all of the feels. Using her experience, practical tips, and the vulnerability of her story, Susan has written a powerful book that is absolutely going to empower women. Her journey and the tools she shares for overcoming adversity and finding success are invaluable. She is unapologetically authentic, and it shines through every page!"

—**Pam Vanderbilt**, Owner and CEO at
Unapologetically You: Living the Diaita Life, LLC;
Integrative Health and Wellness Coach

"This book offers simple tools anyone can use to grow as a leader—all in one place. 'Playing to Win vs. Trying Not to Lose' was my favorite chapter. So glad this book exists to give HOPE to all who are out there trying to figure out their own excellence!"

—**Maggie Newhouse**

"This book is a powerful and uplifting journey that inspires readers to embrace change and trust their inner strength. Its clear, compassionate voice makes even complex ideas feel accessible and encouraging. The author weaves together real-life stories and practical advice in a way that feels both authentic and motivating. I found myself nodding along, smiling, and feeling ready to take action by the end of each chapter. If you're looking for a book that boosts confidence and sparks positive momentum, this one is a must-read!"

—**Kim Sailor**
Bravenly Independent Consultant

WOMEN WIRED TO WIN

The Direct Sales Playbook for Female Entrepreneurs Who Want to Dream Big, Plan Smart, and Find Freedom in Their Business

SUSAN NORMAN

WOMEN WIRED TO WIN

The Direct Sales Playbook for Female Entrepreneurs Who Want to Dream Big, Plan Smart, and Find Freedom in Their Business

For permission requests, speaking inquiries, and bulk order purchase options, visit:

SusanNormanOnline.com

ISBN: 979-8-9935722-1-5 (Paperback)
ISBN: 979-8-9941688-9-9 (Hardcover)

Book Design by Transcendent Publishing
Editing by Lori Lynn Enterprises

Holy Bible, New International Version®, NIV® Copyright ©1973, 1978, 1984, 2011 by Biblica, Inc.® Used by permission. All rights reserved worldwide.

Holy Bible, New Living Translation, (NLT) copyright © 1996, 2004, 2015 by Tyndale House Foundation. Used by permission of Tyndale House Publishers, Inc., Carol Stream, Illinois 60188. All rights reserved.

The Holy Bible, English Standard Version. ESV® Text Edition: 2016. Copyright © 2001 by Crossway Bibles, a publishing ministry of Good News Publishers.

While the principles and strategies shared in this book are designed to inspire and empower you, **no guarantees are made regarding any specific financial or personal results.** The examples and stories shared are for illustrative purposes only and reflect individual experiences. They are not promises of what you will achieve.

Your success depends on many factors—your effort, experience, timing, resources, and the market—and will vary from person to person. Neither the author nor the publisher shall be held responsible or liable for any losses, damages, or results arising from the application of the information in this book.

By reading this book, you acknowledge and accept that you alone are responsible for your own actions, decisions, and results, and that you will seek professional advice as needed for your specific situation.

"For I know the plans I have for you," declares
the LORD, "plans to prosper you and not to harm you,
plans to give you hope and a future."

Jeremiah 29:11 (NIV)

CONTENTS

DEDICATION

This book is dedicated to my family, who have always believed in me, and my friends, who have cheered me on. Most importantly, to my Lord, because without His grace and direction, it wouldn't be possible.

FOREWORD

For over a decade, I have had the absolute privilege of knowing Susan Norman—a woman whose kindness, compassion, and unwavering faith shine through in everything she does. She is one of the most heartfelt, generous, and servant-hearted Christian women I have ever met. Her ability to uplift, encourage, and pour into others is nothing short of inspiring.

And that is exactly what you will find in this book—a reflection of her heart, her wisdom, and her journey.

What sets this book apart is that it's not just another business guide—it's a transformational road map for women entrepreneurs who are ready to break through fear, silence self-doubt, and step into their God-given potential.

The best part? Susan doesn't just teach success from theory—she has lived it. Through challenges, setbacks, and moments of uncertainty, she discovered the power of perseverance, faith, and belief in oneself. She has walked the road of financial struggles, personal hardships, and learning to trust the process. And now, she's handing you the road map to do the same.

Each chapter is filled with not only practical business advice but also deep personal insights that will encourage you to trust yourself, embrace your strengths, and move forward with confidence. If you are ready for a massive transformation and know you deserve more, Susan will show you exactly how to create your dream life.

You'll walk away with a renewed belief in yourself—knowing that you are capable, worthy, and fully equipped to step into the calling placed on your heart.

If you're ready to create the life and business you've been dreaming of, this is where it starts.

To my dear friend Susan—thank you from the bottom of my heart for writing this book for the women who deserve it ALL. You are a true gift to all of us, and especially in my life. I am beyond honored that you asked me to write this foreword. Your wisdom, your strategies, and your heart are simply brilliant.

And to the reader, now is your time. Grab a cup of coffee or tea, turn the page, lean in, and get ready—because my friend, Susan Norman, is about to take you on a life-changing journey.

—Michelle Cunningham
International Bestselling Author of
Do It Anyway, Girl and *You Are a Million Dollar Brand*

HUMBLE BEGINNINGS

We were broke. Not the "cut back on lattes" kind of broke, but the kind that meant choosing between rent and groceries.

I remember staring at a stack of unpaid bills that were piling up faster than the dirty laundry, feeling like a failure. No matter how many times I added, subtracted, or stretched every last dollar, the numbers never worked in our favor.

As a young, stay-at-home mom with two babies under two, I wanted so badly to help provide for my family. My husband, Corbit, was already working two jobs, and we were barely keeping our heads above water.

Honestly, it felt like we were drowning in basic living expenses. Every day felt heavier than the last, and every bill that arrived in the mail was yet another reminder that we were slipping further behind.

We had one car—and even that payment was a stretch—so getting a second one? Totally out of the question. Back then, before the internet was what it is today, the thought of working from home was as far-fetched as Cinderella's fairy godmother turning a pumpkin into a chariot.

Every morning, I'd sit at our refinished, hand-me-down kitchen table, sipping lukewarm coffee and feeling helpless. I had to find a solution. But what? How could I help?

My mind raced, trying to come up with something—anything— but no matter how optimistic I was, my options always felt limited.

I remember flipping through the classifieds, scanning the want-ads. (You know, those old-school paper ads we used for job hunting before Google made everything searchable in, literally, two seconds. Ah, the good ol' days.)

Every single listing seemed to require skills or experience I just didn't have. I'd ask myself, "Seriously? Do I need a PhD in rocket science just to get an entry-level job?" Frustration turned into hopelessness. I wasn't qualified for anything.

And then one day, out of nowhere, a recommendation came my way.

A family friend suggested I contact her niece, who was making waves in a direct sales company. I didn't know much about direct sales at the time, but I figured, *What do I have to lose?* Despite my initial reservations, I found myself calling her number, hop-ing—praying—this might be the answer I'd been waiting for.

I can still vividly recall that first phone call with Debbie. My heart pounded as I waited for her to answer, completely unaware that this one call—this one conversation—would change the course of my life forever.

Naturally, my polite manners (that had been drilled into me since childhood) kicked in, and I greeted her with, "Hi, Mrs. Leflar, I got your number from your aunt about a work-from-home business opportunity."

To my surprise (and slight embarrassment) she laughed! Then she said in the sweetest voice, "You don't have to call me Mrs. or ma'am, you can call me Debbie."

And just like that, my direct sales journey began.

Despite being shy, inexperienced, and full of uncertainty, I was also brimming with hope and a strong desire to learn. I had no clue how I was going to make this work, or where I'd find customers. But I was too naïve to let doubt steal my dreams.

Or, as I like to say, "I was too dumb to doubt."

I didn't know what I didn't know, but I was driven by a single dream—to create a better future for my family, and I was armed with an unshakable determination to succeed.

Through my ignorance and fear, I held onto this promise from Isaiah 41:10 (NIV): Do not fear, for I am with you; do not be dismayed, for I am your God. I will strengthen you and help you; I will uphold you with my righteous right hand.

Even when I couldn't see how it was all going to work out, I clung to the belief that God's presence was bigger than my fear. That truth kept me moving when everything in me wanted to quit.

**It's not where you start—it's where you finish
that counts the most.**

I started out as a timid, introverted girl who would burst into tears over a late library book and could barely speak up in a room full of people, but I somehow managed to earn a car in my first 10 weeks in that direct sales business—and that was just the beginning!

From that moment on, over the next 30 years and through several direct sales ventures, I was able to grow an incredible team and rank in the top 1.5% in my company.

This journey not only helped us get ahead financially but it also led to earning the use of numerous company cars, winning a ton of prizes (like diamonds and trips) and creating countless unforgettable memories with my girlfriends.

What started out as a way to help pay for rent and groceries has turned into a mission centered on personal and professional development.

From Pitiful to Profitable

When people learn I'm a top producer, they assume I must have been a natural at sales. Ha! I wish I could say that was true. It would have been a lot less painful and saved me a whole lot of embarrassment.

But before I became a rockstar in direct sales, I was pretty pitiful.

At 15 years old, I landed my first "sales" job alongside one of my best girlfriends. It was a commission-based telemarketing job for an organization called Children's Rights of America.

On our first day, we walked into the office, excited but nervous, not knowing exactly what to expect. The lighting was dim, and the room smelled like cigarette smoke, fast food, and stale coffee.

You could hear the chatter of dozens of voices, which sounded to me like a room full of nasally valley girls. I mean, this was the '80s after all. I'm not gonna lie—I may have even asked myself, "Is this legit?" But I was determined to give it my best shot.

We were guided to our stations, handed a script, a list of names, and a phone. The goal? Call people and sell pizzas and cookies, with part of the proceeds going to charity to help children. I thought, *This is going to be great! I can help a good cause, and make some easy money!* Boy, was I wrong.

Call after call, and rejection after rejection, my excitement soon faded as I listened to people yell at me, hang up on me, or simply say no. I remember leaving that first day feeling super frustrated and thinking, *Whoa, that was rough! Will every day be like this? I don't know if I can put myself through that again.* But I wasn't giving up. No way! I was willing and eager to learn.

I tried everything—from mimicking *how* other people were talking to tweaking my sales pitch. Nope, that didn't work either.

After three days of *zero* sales, I got called into the manager's office.

They let me go.

Apparently, keeping me around was costing them more than cutting their losses. Ouch. I hadn't sold a single pizza or cookie after what felt like hundreds of phone calls. You'd think I was trying to break some kind of record for least sales ever!

It's funny looking back now because who would've thought that the quiet, shy 15-year-old who got fired from her first job would one day build multiple successful direct sales businesses over different seasons of life, earning more than a dozen free cars, countless trips and prizes, top leadership titles, and recognition in the top 1.5% of her field?

It wasn't an easy road. I failed—a lot. But every failure taught me something valuable.

If I could go back and tell that 15-year-old version of me that it's all going to work out, I would. I would tell her to stop worrying about perfection, to embrace the mistakes, and to trust that those tough moments would build the strength she needed later.

Because if I had let that first sales job define me, it would have stopped me from pursuing my first direct sales business when I was just 19 with two babies at home (Kaela, who was 19 months old, and Autumn, a mere three months) and building my dream career.

Baby Kaela, my husband Corbit, baby Autumn, and nineteen-year-old me—Corbit and I were just babies ourselves!

Looking back on it all, I'm honestly so grateful for everything I've experienced, and I'm proud of who I've become because of it. I wouldn't change a single thing—each step, even the tough ones, played a part in shaping the person I am today.

Why This Book? Why Now?

After over 30 years in direct sales and mastering the ins and outs of the business, I now specialize in helping others WIN BIG in the industry.

If you've ever thought, *Can I really do this? What if I fail?*—you're not alone. I've been there. I know the doubts, the fear, the frustration of feeling stuck. And I made a promise to myself: **If I ever figured it out, I'd share it with others.** That's exactly what I'm doing here.

While I'm still connected to the world of direct sales because I genuinely love the products, the people, and the industry, my primary focus now is building my independent sales and consulting brand, Women Wired to Win.

In the last two years, I've generated nearly $4 million in personal sales revenue, working as a high-ticket closer and independent contractor to help coaches and business owners sell their premium offers. I also coach direct sellers and network marketers on how to build profitable businesses and brand themselves confidently online.

This book is the road map I wish I had when I was getting started. It will help you pinpoint exactly where you are, where you want to be, and how to bridge the gap between the two. No fluff. No waiting for the "perfect" moment. Just proven and results-driven strategies to move you forward.

Every chapter is packed with practical steps that you can implement immediately. You'll begin transforming your mindset and habits from day one, bringing you closer to the success you deserve.

Beyond the Book—Where Sisters Win Together

This book and the *Women Wired to Win* podcast are just the beginning. Real change happens when you don't walk the journey alone. That's why I created the **Women Wired to Win Community**—a place where we go deeper together, apply these principles in real life, and celebrate every step forward.

Inside, you'll find women who believe in you, encourage you, and hold you up when the road feels hard. You'll also receive:

- Weekly encouragement and live training to keep you inspired
- Early access to new tools, workshops, and courses
- A circle of like-minded women who are aligned in purpose and cheering for your success

If you're ready to put these ideas into practice, to become the woman you know you're called to be, and to finally turn your dreams into reality—this is your invitation.

Together, we're stronger. And I'm ready to help you win.

Find your sisterhood of support by going to:

community.womenwiredtowin.com

PLAYING TO WIN VS. TRYING NOT TO LOSE

There's a moment in every woman's business journey when she has to make a choice.

Play it safe—or play to win.

For me, that moment came a few years into my direct sales journey. I was sitting in my office, staring at a stack of bills we couldn't pay, and crying on the phone with a trusted friend.

We had bought our first single-family home only the year before—what should have been a dream-come-true moment. But instead, reality hit like a freight train.

My husband and I were way over our heads financially, buying far more house than we could afford, and we were on the brink of foreclosure. (*What I call our "young and dumb" era.*) Things were tough.

To say I was overwhelmed is putting it mildly.

We were stuck between a rock and a hard place: give up and lose everything, or fight to turn things around.

I wasn't ready to give up. Not by a long shot.

While all that was happening in the background, I had just gotten started in a new direct sales business, hoping to make some headway to help yet again.

The only problem? I didn't have the inventory I needed to grow or the money to buy it. And the people closest to me? They thought I was crazy for even *considering* putting more money into something that hadn't "proven" itself yet.

They didn't see what I saw.

I saw possibility.

And in that moment—scared, desperate, but full of fire—I took a massive leap of faith and made a decision that changed everything.

Even though our credit was tanking, somehow, through my husband's credit union, we managed to get a loan.

Not for furniture. Not for food. Not to pay off a bill.

But to invest in *me*. In my business. In our future.

It was a risk—no doubt about it—but I believed in what I was doing. I believed in *me*.

That, my friend, is what it looks like to *play to win*.

Playing to Win Looks Different

Playing to win isn't about being reckless. It's not about ignoring responsibilities or making impulsive decisions. It's about deciding—deep in your gut—that you're done playing small.

When you're trying not to lose instead of playing to win, your whole business shifts into survival mode:

- You only post when you feel like it.
- You avoid the hard conversations.
- You don't invite people to join your team because you're afraid they'll say no.
- You talk yourself out of going to events, trainings, or conferences because "you can't afford it."

But let's be honest—can you really afford *not* to?

Playing to win means betting on yourself before anyone else does. It means going first, leading with courage, and showing up with conviction. It means pushing past what feels safe and stepping into what's possible.

I wasn't playing defense anymore. I wasn't asking, *"What if this doesn't work?"* I was declaring, *"This WILL work because I'm going to make it work."*

The Power of Going All In

That loan I took out? It was terrifying. But it forced me to show up differently. I had skin in the game now. Failure wasn't an option—not because it magically became easy, but because I was too invested to quit.

I worked smarter. I followed up. I made the calls. I hosted the events, even when only two people showed up. I learned. I grew. I got better.

And within 14 months, I had earned the use of a company car. I landed in the top 1.5% of my company. And you know what else? We saved our house. We kept our dream alive.

All because I chose to play to win.

Not coast. Not wait. Not hope something would happen.

I *made it* happen.

The Mindset Shift That Changed My Life

Trying not to lose feels safe. It feels responsible. But really? It's a slow death to your dreams.

When you operate from fear—of failing, of judgment, of wasting time or money—you stay stuck in the same cycle. Hoping. Waiting. Wishing.

But when you decide to play to win?

You show up differently. You start trusting yourself. You stop looking for signs and start *creating* them.

You don't just dream. You *do*.

What Playing to Win Looks Like in Your Business

For you, playing to win might not look like taking out a loan—but it *will* require a bold move.

Maybe it's finally committing to consistent action, even when it's uncomfortable.

Maybe it's investing in a training or mentorship, even when it stretches your budget.

Maybe it's going live for the first time, even if your hands shake the whole time.

Maybe it's showing up fully, even when no one's clapping yet.

Because here's the truth: When you play to win, the scoreboard doesn't always reflect your effort right away. But the game changes the moment *you* do.

If You've Been Playing Small, This Is Your Wake-Up Call

You're not here to just "get by" in business.

You're here to *build* something. To make a difference. To create options for your family. To rewrite your story. To rise up and say, *"I am capable. I am called. And I'm going all in."*

So today, ask yourself honestly:

- Where have I been playing it safe?
- What would it look like if I played to win starting right now?

It might be scary. It might feel risky. But it will always be worth it.

And if you're still on the fence, wondering if you're "ready" ...

Let me be the one to tell you:

You already are.

You've got everything you need inside of you to win.

All that's left is the decision.

Key Takeaways to WIN

- **Shift from "playing not to lose" to "playing to win."** Stop coasting in your comfort zone. To grow and succeed, you need to take risks, push boundaries, and go after what you really want.

- **Embrace your full potential**. Believe in your unique skills and talents. Don't let fear or self-doubt hold you back. Step up, set bigger goals, and go after them with confidence. You've got what it takes!

- **Overcome challenges with confidence**. Every setback is just a setup for a comeback. Like Babe Ruth said, "Every strikeout brings you closer to a home run." Embrace challenges, learn from them, and keep pushing forward. Your breakthrough is just around the corner!

I Dare You to Take Action

I dare you to play to win.

You've heard the difference between trying not to lose and playing to win, and now it's time to put that mindset into action. Playing to win isn't about staying safe—it's about taking risks, pushing your limits, and going after what you truly want in your business.

Ask yourself:

- What have I been doing to just stay afloat instead of aiming for the win?
- What risks am I avoiding because of fear or self-doubt?
- How can I step up and challenge myself to go after bigger goals?

Here's your challenge:

Pick one area in your business where you've been playing it safe. Whether it's making a big decision, having a tough conversation, or taking a risk—commit to taking bold action today. Don't wait for everything to be perfect. Just go for it!

Remember, nothing changes if nothing changes. And if you want to see a real transformation in your business, you've got to make a move. So, I dare you—stop treading water. Go all in, take the shot, and play to win. The reward is worth the risk.

WINNING THROUGH ACTIVITY

When I was a newbie in sales, not gonna lie—I was scared.

Reaching out to people, handling rejection, and feeling like I was just throwing spaghetti at the wall, hoping something would stick, was intimidating.

But then something shifted.

I realized that every single "no" was actually getting me closer to a "yes." And every yes meant I was one step closer to my dreams.

You see, I used to think success was about talent, luck, or just having the right connections. But you know what it really comes down to?

Math. Yep! **Success isn't magical; it's mathematical.** (*No matter what anyone else says.*)

In other words, it's a numbers game, and that totally made sense to me. I didn't resist it—I *got* it. If I could track the numbers, I could track the growth.

Because here's the truth: Numbers don't lie—and they're predictable.

People, though? They're unpredictable. They *will* disappoint you. Some will cancel. Some won't follow through. Some will say *yes* today and *ghost* you tomorrow.

But here's what I learned: I couldn't control what they did. What *could* I control?

My activity.

Once I stopped stressing about *who* would say yes and started focusing on *how many* people I reached out to, everything changed.

The frustration, the stuck feeling, began to fade. Not because I suddenly became a sales genius or got lucky, but because I committed to showing up and taking action. Every single day.

I stopped obsessing over outcomes and started focusing on my actions. I love a good formula and strategy because they bring clarity and direction.

And once I saw *math* rather than *luck*, it all made sense. With strategy, I could turn my vision into achievable goals. I just had to **trust the numbers.**

Turning Goals Into a Game Plan

For example, when I set my sights on earning my next car, I didn't just sit around hoping it would magically show up in my driveway.

Nope, I made it happen! I made a plan based on the numbers.

I learned that reaching out to 10 people every single day (that's 300 a month) was a proven formula for hitting my goal in six months.

So, I committed. No matter what, I reached out to 10 people every day.

Some days were amazing. Some days were slow. But I stuck with it. And you know what? The odds were in my favor. Because I had an activity goal—not an outcome goal.

Sure enough, I hit my goal.

The Power of What You Can Control

Now, don't get me wrong, goals are super important, but you can't necessarily control the outcome.

I couldn't control how much people spent with me or who joined my team, but I could control how many people I reached out to and how much effort I put into serving them. And that shift in perspective was huge for me.

I started focusing on daily Income Producing Activities (IPAs)—the things within my control, and I started seeing results. Every call, every message, every follow-up built my confidence.

Even when I didn't see immediate wins, each action was like a brick in the foundation of something bigger.

Surprised by my progress, I thought, *Wait … how did I get so good at this?*

Then I remembered that the more people I connected with, the more opportunities I created to win. Rather than stressing about specific sales targets, I set activity goals on what I could control—the actions I could take daily.

> **"Commit your work to the Lord, and your plans will be established."** Proverbs 16:3 (ESV)

When I aligned my actions with purpose, building my business became a process I could enjoy—one step at a time.

A Marathon, Not a Sprint

I have to admit that at the beginning of my journey, I thought I could sprint to success. Work hard for a few months, push through, and boom—everything would fall into place.

But success doesn't work like that.

Think about a marathon runner. Their goal is to cross the finish line, sure.

But what actually gets them there? It's not just the goal, it's the **daily discipline**. The early morning runs, the relentless training, and the commitment to keep going even when it's tough. That's what separates those who almost make it from those who *do*.

You see: Success—whether in business, personal growth, or any big dream—comes from focusing on the daily actions we take and the effort we put in, day in and day out. While vision and goals set the direction, it's the consistent work that moves us forward.

You can't rush the process or skip the work. It's like trying to finish a marathon without training first—you'll burn out before the halfway mark.

When I stopped fixating on the outcome and started focusing on the daily activity instead, I felt stronger and more confident because I was in control of something. Suddenly, success wasn't some final destination anymore—it became a journey I actually enjoyed being on.

So, whether you're starting a business, chasing a goal, or working on your next big thing, remember: it's not about sprinting to the finish line. It's about **putting in the work and trusting the process.**

Success Is a Series of Small Steps

What I've come to realize on this 30-year journey is that success isn't one big, dramatic leap—one big break, one major moment, and suddenly you've made it.

The truth?

Success is built on a thousand small steps in the right direction.

As I continued to show up consistently, day after day, week after week, for those small windows of focused activity, I began to see more progress.

Every call, every conversation, every new customer, every new team member—they were all tiny victories that built momentum.

That gave me the energy to keep pushing forward.

I stopped worrying about whether or not people would buy or join my team. Instead, I focused on my daily activities. and before long, the results began to follow.

And that's the real secret.

It's about showing up consistently, even when the going gets tough.

"Let us not become weary in doing good, for at the proper time we will reap a harvest if we do not give up." Galatians 6:9 (NIV)

When you focus on activity, the results will come.

They always come.

Key Takeaways to WIN

- **Success is indeed a numbers game.** The more people you connect with, the greater your chances for success.

- **Enjoy the journey.** It's not just about the outcome—enjoy the process and impact you're making.

- **Consistency is key.** Every effort counts. Keep reaching out with sincerity and passion.

- **Trust the process.** Every connection matters. Your dedication will lead to success in unexpected, inspiring ways.

I Dare You to Take Action

I dare you to focus on the activity.

Instead of stressing about outcomes, commit to a daily action plan. The more people you connect with, the more opportunities you create. When you focus on the activity and trust the process, the results will follow.

Ask yourself:

- Which specific outcome can I put into motion?
- How many people will I reach out to today?
- What is one action I can take to move toward my goal?

Here's your challenge:

Set an activity goal. Track your numbers. Keep count of your daily efforts. Show up, day in and day out. Stay consistent. Whether you hear a yes, no, or maybe, just keep going. Every effort adds up.

Success isn't magic, it's math.

PEOPLE OVER PROFITS

Walking into a routine doctor's appointment at the Children's Hospital on July 2, 2012, which also happened to be my birthday, I came face-to-face with a profound challenge.

My youngest daughter and I unexpectedly bumped into our dearest friends and their daughter. Our families had grown incredibly close over the years—our daughters were more like sisters than friends.

That's when they shared their heartbreaking news. Taby, their precious 18-year-old daughter, who had been battling brain cancer since childhood, had experienced a recurrence.

Her little body was rapidly deteriorating, despite numerous surgeries, and by the end of November, she was sent home on hospice care. The doctors said she had only days or weeks left to live.

Wanting to minimize the involvement of hospice services, the family hoped to provide Taby with a sense of normalcy by surrounding her with familiar faces.

They had no close relatives nearby, so we became inseparable, devoting ourselves to caring for her and her family during her last months. Our commitment was so deep that I was entrusted with administering her end-of-life hospice medication to keep her comfortable.

On December 11, 2012, Taby took her last breath, finding peace in the arms of Jesus. We will forever cherish the privilege of being there for her and her family during that time.

I share this story because it forced me to make a decision—one that I knew could have significant consequences for my business. Despite the potential risks, I chose to take two months off to support our friends during their time of need—to prioritize people over profits.

Looking back, I would make the same choice without hesitation.

A Life-Altering Call

Fast forward a couple of weeks to January 2013, smack dab in the middle of our company's area midyear retreat. That's when I got *the call*—you know, the kind that rocks your world and changes everything.

The news? Our team had missed our unit production requirement for two months straight, and just like that, I was asked to step down as a leader.

Seven years of blood, sweat, and tears building a unit, supporting other women, and boom—suddenly I'm out. Talk about a gut punch. I kept asking myself, "How did this happen?"

At first, I was mad. Then hurt. But when I finally took an honest look at the situation, two things hit me:

1. If this had been a regular job, I would've been straight-up fired.

2. If our unit had been truly healthy, my two-month absence wouldn't have tanked things.

That second realization? Total game-changer. Right then, I decided to focus on building stronger systems, better training, smart automation, and real duplication. I needed my business and team to run smoothly—even when I wasn't there.

This led me to discover online attraction marketing. After taking a year off from team building to focus on my customers, I jumped back in beginning February 2014 with a mission to rebuild my unit. Bigger, stronger, better—that was the plan.

I hit some major resistance (hardly anyone in my industry was using social media or video back then), but I saw the potential and went all in. I became obsessed with learning—boot camp after boot camp, strategy after strategy.

I remember hunting for mass texting apps before they were even a thing. Yeah, I was "that girl," ahead of the curve way before it was cool.

The options were super limited back then. Even with the "fancy" customized text features, I still had to hit "send" hundreds of times. Not exactly convenient, but way better than copy/pasting one text at a time!

Through trial and error, I stumbled onto some game-changing tools for mass calling, texting, and email automations. It wasn't pretty at first, but these tools turned out to be exactly what I needed.

With these automation tricks up my sleeve, we rebuilt our team from practically nothing to the top 1.5% of our company in just seven months. Not too shabby, right?

Redefining Business

One of the biggest reasons I took on the challenge of rebuilding my business was to show my daughters that setbacks aren't the end. They saw me fall, but they also saw me rise, stronger than before.

I wanted them to understand that adversity isn't something to fear; it's an opportunity for growth. We can always rebuild—and rebuild better.

Losing my leadership title was a tough pill to swallow, but it taught me something important—my knowledge and expertise live within me. No title defines who I am as a leader or as a person. That experience reminded me that true leadership isn't about position—it's about service.

"The greatest among you shall be your servant."
Matthew 23:11 (ESV)

After losing my title, I was no longer invited to train or speak at our weekly team success events, as if all my knowledge and experience had vanished overnight.

Feeling that level of exclusion shifted my perspective. I promised myself that if I ever built again, my approach to leadership would be completely different. I would create an inclusive environment where every team member's strengths are seen, valued, and leveraged.

My mission became clear: **Use my business to build people—not use people to build my business.**

I committed to empowering other women in our organization, giving them space to share their gifts, lead trainings, and step into the spotlight.

Successful entrepreneurs genuinely care about people. That kind of passion, paired with a focus on long-term success, helps businesses thrive. Without it, success is often short-lived because people can spot insincerity from a mile away.

Looking back, my journey has taught me invaluable lessons about putting people first, facing challenges head-on, and empowering others. Through hard work and a daily commitment to growth, I haven't just rebuilt my career—I've created a culture rooted in real connection and shared success.

Key Takeaways to WIN

- **Put people first.** Always choose to help and support people, even if it means making sacrifices.
- **Facing challenges.** This can teach you to bounce back stronger, rethink your plans, and discover new ways to succeed. So, when things get tough, embrace them as opportunities to learn and grow.
- **Learning from setbacks.** After a setback, I learned that building a strong team and helping others succeed is more important than just meeting goals.
- **Perseverance pays off.** Even when things are tough, keep going! By learning new things and trying different ways, you can achieve big successes.
- **Empowering others.** Instead of just leading, empower others to share their skills and ideas. Together, you can accomplish more and make a positive impact.

I Dare You to Take Action

I dare you to prioritize people over profits.

In a world driven by numbers and bottom lines, it's easy to forget what truly fuels long-term success: people. Your team. Your customers. Your community. When you put people first, profits naturally follow.

Ask yourself:

- Am I investing time in building real relationships?
- Are my decisions supporting the people behind the numbers?
- How could I better support my community?

Here's your challenge:

This week, take one action that puts people first. Reach out to a team member to offer mentorship, apply customer feedback to improve their experience, or support a local cause.

When you invest in people, you build stronger relationships. That's when your business becomes not only successful but also deeply fulfilling.

AUTOMATE TO ACCELERATE

As you can imagine, relinquishing my title as a leader after my unit had failed to hit our production goal for two months in a row (while I cared for my honorary daughter during the final weeks of her young life) was grueling, but I had a decision to make. Either stay down in the valley or rise up and climb that mountain again.

I remember feeling really frustrated—and, to be honest, very angry—for a couple of months. I dug my heels in and thought, *You know what? I'm just going to take care of my customers right now. I'll support them, service them, and that's it!*

Then I faced another decision. I could choose to remain bitter, or I could choose to get better. I chose to get better because deep down, I knew I would eventually get myself up, dust myself off, and get moving again. But first, I needed to be ready and ensure that this time, I had the right systems in place.

So, I got moving.

Finding Inspiration

I did boot camp after boot camp with an unquenchable thirst for knowledge, devouring all the info I could about building online. One day, I found myself on YouTube, watching a video, when I came across a gal who, it turns out, was from the same company as me. She was funny, smart, and working her business in a way I wanted to learn!

She became a silent mentor of mine, even though she didn't realize it at the time. I followed her closely, watching what she was doing, and eventually, I reached out to her, though it took me a couple of years! And that silent mentor all those years ago is the very same person who wrote the foreword of my book! I mean, how cool is that?

I learned a lot from her, and I decided to build my business on my terms. I was determined to build something big in the online world, reaching more people.

I felt like I was shouting from the rooftops, but no one in my leadership was listening. Honestly, they thought I was nuts. They even asked me to prayerfully *stop* what I was doing (genuinely thinking they were helping me with this advice), all the way up until 2020 when the world changed, COVID happened, and everything shut down.

Thank God I was ready! Because I had planned, prepared, and put systems in place, it didn't affect me. While everyone else was scrambling to keep their business afloat and learning this online virtual world, I had already been working that way for a few years.

Would you believe I did $10,000 more in personal sales in 2020 than I did in 2019? When face-to-face parties disappeared for a while, I had online systems in place. Even more than before, other consultants and leaders began reaching out to me for help with streaming live, hosting virtual parties successfully, creating automations, and so much more.

Embracing Change

I saw this shift happening more than ten years ago, around 2014, when people were using social media in powerful ways. So I chose to embrace it, learn, and get better every day. This took me from one of my worst years ever in 2014—it was really a struggle—to a thriving business.

I found inspiration from Michelle Cunningham, my online mentor, and got into action. I thought, *If there's a way to do X, Y, and Z easier, I'm going to figure it out.*

Gradually, I began to put systems in place, do automations, and stretch myself with video and live streaming—way before Facebook had its live feature!

Remember Periscope on Twitter? Yeah, I was there because that was the only way you could go live at that time. I also used YouTube, recording videos on my phone and uploading them for my team.

In the process of learning these systems and strategies, I grew a tremendous business in 2018 despite it being the sickest year of my life, which landed me in the hospital. I even ended up needing an urgent surgery at the end of our business year.

Even though I faced significant health challenges that year, I was still able to lead my team to "Most Improved Unit" in our entire state. It was a *huge* honor, especially because it meant we had the largest percentage of growth compared to any other unit within our company in the state.

Not only that, but I was also humbled to achieve several milestones that year, including ranking as the number one recruiter in my national area, coming in at number two in personal sales, ranking third in team unit sales across the national area, and being recognized with the title of "Best All Around."

Each of these accomplishments was a result of the hard work and dedication of my team and me, and I remain incredibly grateful for the opportunities to have grown alongside such talented women.

Rising After Every Fall

Although you might find yourself in valley moments, as I have, the key is not to give up. You've got to keep going, stretching, learning, and growing. You've got to keep your "why" in front of you. For me, that was security for my family. It was also about showing my girls that their mom could fall down but pick herself up and keep going until she reached her dreams.

That year proved something powerful—I went from being at my worst physically to achieving my absolute best year in business. The crucial lesson: build systems while you're able, so they can work for you when you're not.

Online systems and resources became a key part of creating success in my business over the last ten years. I was determined to figure things out and make my life easier. Whatever I needed to do, I was willing to take the time, so that others wouldn't have to go through the same frustrations I did—including literally falling down a flight of stairs.

Years ago, in one of my former direct sales businesses, I was finishing up a party. I had two enormous bags filled with all my kit products, and I was eager to head home. This was a townhome that had two long flights of stairs just to get to the front door.

As I was leaving, my feet decided it was time for a little surprise party, and, of course, I was the guest of honor. I was holding onto those giant bags for dear life as if somehow that was gonna save me, and that's when I knew I was about to take a very dramatic tumble. And boy, did I ever!

I went tumbling down those stairs, like somehow I missed the memo about gravity. When I finally hit the ground, all I wanted to do was disappear—preferably under a rock, or maybe a whole mountain!

Despite the pain and the embarrassment, I managed to get up, make an awkward joke, and laugh it off. The drive home was excruciating, and when I looked at my legs, they were all skinned up, covered in cuts and bruises, with my pantyhose ripped to shreds.

In business, you're going to experience your own falls—moments when you feel like you've tumbled down a flight of steps. It might not be an actual physical event, but it will sting just as much. The key is to rise up, shake it off, and keep pressing on.

From Systems to Brand

Success isn't about avoiding setbacks—it's about building a foundation that helps you rise every time you fall. I could have either stayed where I was—frustrated, exhausted, and stuck—or I could take everything I had learned and move forward with a new mindset.

Whether you're starting from scratch or scaling to new heights, the key is working smarter, not harder. That's why I became obsessed with automation, online systems, and strategies that would allow me to grow my business without running myself into the ground.

I didn't want to be tied to my phone 24/7. I wanted freedom. Freedom to spend time with my family, to enjoy life, and to know that my business was still thriving even when I needed to step away. And that's exactly what automation allowed me to do.

The truth is, systems are what separate struggle from success. When life throws you curveballs (and trust me, it will), having the right systems and tools in place means your business keeps moving forward, even when you need to pause. I had built a foundation that could withstand life's ups and downs, and it made all the difference.

But … there was still one missing piece. *Me.*

While I had figured out how to run my business online, I started to realize that automation alone wasn't enough. People weren't just buying products; they were buying trust, connection, and authenticity. I needed to show up in a way that made people feel like they knew me.

It was time to take things a step further. It was time to build something bigger than just a business.

It was time to build a brand.

Key Takeaways to WIN

- **Systems make success easier**. Set up tools and automation to work smarter, not harder. See my Top 10 Systems for Success in the Bonus Content section at the end of this book.

- **Adapt to change**. Embrace new methods, like building an online brand, to stay ahead in your business.

- **Prepare for the unexpected**. Planning and setting up systems ahead of time can help you thrive when things change unexpectedly.

- **Resilience is key**. Falling down is inevitable, but the ability to get back up and keep going is what leads to success.

I Dare You to Take Action

I dare you to automate.

You've just learned the power of systems and automation to move your business forward, especially when life throws challenges your way. Now it's time to act.

Ask yourself:

- What's draining my time?
- What could run without me?
- Where could I create more impact with less stress?

Here's your challenge:

Identify one area of your business that needs support, and automate it this week. That might look like setting up email follow-ups, scheduling your content, or building a simple recruiting funnel that works even when you're offline. Don't wait for everything to be perfect. Start imperfectly and refine as you go.

Success doesn't come from working harder. It comes from working smarter. Build the systems, streamline the process, and watch your business accelerate.

Want an all-in-one solution to automate your marketing, organize your leads, and help your business run more smoothly? Check out the platform I use (and recommend) at:

info.BuildItBig.io

BUILD A TRUSTED PERSONAL BRAND

I had once again hit a plateau, and it was frustrating. I knew I had the drive, the knowledge, and the work ethic, but I couldn't break through to the next level. I saw so many people doing the same thing—posting product photos and copying corporate marketing scripts, hoping someone would bite. There had to be a better way!

During my rebuilding stage, I researched top leaders in direct sales and network marketing. They all had something in common: **They were building an online brand for themselves, *not* just promoting their company!**

In fact, you had to be a private investigator to even figure out which company they represented. Some of them, to this day, I still don't know. But one thing was clear: the industry was shifting, and I needed to evolve with it.

That's when I had an "aha" moment that changed everything. I had been so focused on selling a product and working the system that I had completely overlooked the most important piece of the puzzle: *Me.*

I realized that building a personal brand online was the missing link to even bigger growth! In a space where so many people sell the same products, what set me apart wasn't my company—it was me.

I needed to stop being just a salesperson and start being a brand. Because no one can be YOU better than YOU!

You Are the Brand

At the time, I was expecting my first grandbaby, and it was such a special season of life. So I wanted my brand to reflect more than just makeup—it needed to speak to women who were going through similar stages in life, like me.

I asked myself: *What's important to me right now? What do I need? What do the women around me need?* The answers were clear: women in my life were looking for practical solutions for maturing skin, everyday makeup looks, and something that felt real and achievable.

That's when **"Susan Norman, The Makeup Mimi"** was born. "Mimi" wasn't just a catchy name—it was a reflection of warmth, love, and care. It made my brand personal and approachable. I wasn't just a consultant; I was someone who understood women balancing it all and looking for simple, effective ways to feel confident.

At first, I had my doubts … *Would anyone care? Would they even show up when I was LIVE? Would they actually listen to what I had to say?* But over time, I started to see something amazing happen.

By sharing my story, I became more than just a consultant; I became a friend. I wasn't just selling makeup anymore. I was building *relationships* and genuinely helping my audience solve their skin care problems.

I focused on showing up in a way that was fun and actually meaningful. I went live with tutorials, hosted exciting weekly events, and made my audience the priority.

And you know what? Slowly but surely, people began to show up, and my audience grew. What I realized is **people don't just buy products—they buy into YOU**—your story, your values, and how you show up to help them.

> **"Commit to the LORD whatever you do, and he will establish your plans."** Proverbs 16:3 (NIV)

The Riches Are in the Niches

Growing your business means reaching as many people as possible. But how do you get in front of *lots* and *lots* of people?

It's definitely not by shouting all over social media, "buy my stuff," or filling up Facebook feeds with what looks like an endless stream of infomercials, hoping to find the right prospects. (I mean, who wants to scroll through that?)

To grow bigger, you've got to get smaller. The more specific you get, the more powerful your impact. **If you're trying to speak to everyone, you're actually speaking to no one.**

You might think, *"But if I only focus on a small group of people, won't I limit my potential?"* Actually, no! By narrowing in on those who need what you have, they're more likely to connect with you, engage with your content, and let's be honest—BUY from you!

So, *how do we reach a larger audience by focusing on a smaller one?*

Your niche is the answer! When you focus on a specific audience, you attract the right people, not just anyone. Your message speaks directly to those who want what you offer.

In other words, **the riches are in the niches.**

My niche was *women who were looking for practical solutions for maturing skin and everyday makeup looks to feel more confident.*

I remember selling 100 mascaras in one day during a new mascara launch with my former direct sales company, and it wasn't because I was screaming "BUY NOW" all over social media. It was because I posted a side-by-side picture of *me*—not a stock photo, not a celebrity, but *me*. I shared my personal experience, my excitement, and why I loved the product.

The right people connected with me because it felt authentic, honest, and relatable. That's the power of niching down.

You don't have to shrink your audience; just speak directly to those who truly need what you offer, addressing their needs and pain points, rather than wasting time trying to reach everyone.

Think of it like a camera lens—when you focus on one thing, everything else blurs into the background. That's how you create content that stands out.

Show Up Big to Build Trust

John Maxwell says it best: **"The secret of your success is found in your daily routine."**

Trust isn't built overnight. It's built through consistent action, showing up when people expect you, and being a steady presence online.

Ever heard that saying, *"Slow and steady wins the race"*? It's true.

Just like the tortoise outpaced the hare, small, consistent actions will always outshine bursts of excitement that fizzle out after a week. Sure, the hare was fast, but he didn't keep at it—he got distracted, took a nap, and lost the race. Meanwhile, the tortoise kept going. He was steady, persistent, and most importantly, *consistent*.

Whether it's social media posts, emails, weekly live events, or team training, showing up when people expect you—and doing it regularly—is how you build trust.

Let me just say, I *get it*. I know what it feels like to wonder if all your hard work is even making a difference.

I've been there.

When I started my Makeup Mimi Monday live videos, I had fewer than 50 followers on my business page. Some days, it felt like I was talking to myself. I kept showing up and reminded myself that even if no one was watching live, the replays could still reach someone.

Did I always feel like doing it? *Nope.*

Were there days when not a single person was watching? *Oh yeah.*

Week after week, month after month, I would show up and go live for my signature show, Makeup Mimi Monday. And that's when I saw the change happen. My audience grew, my engagement increased, and my customers began to see me as the go-to person for beauty advice. Not because I had the perfect setup or flawless videos, but because I was reliable.

People buy from those they know, like, and trust. If you ghost your audience for weeks at a time, they'll move on to someone who shows up consistently. But when you're steady—even when life gets busy, even when it's inconvenient—you build credibility that lasts.

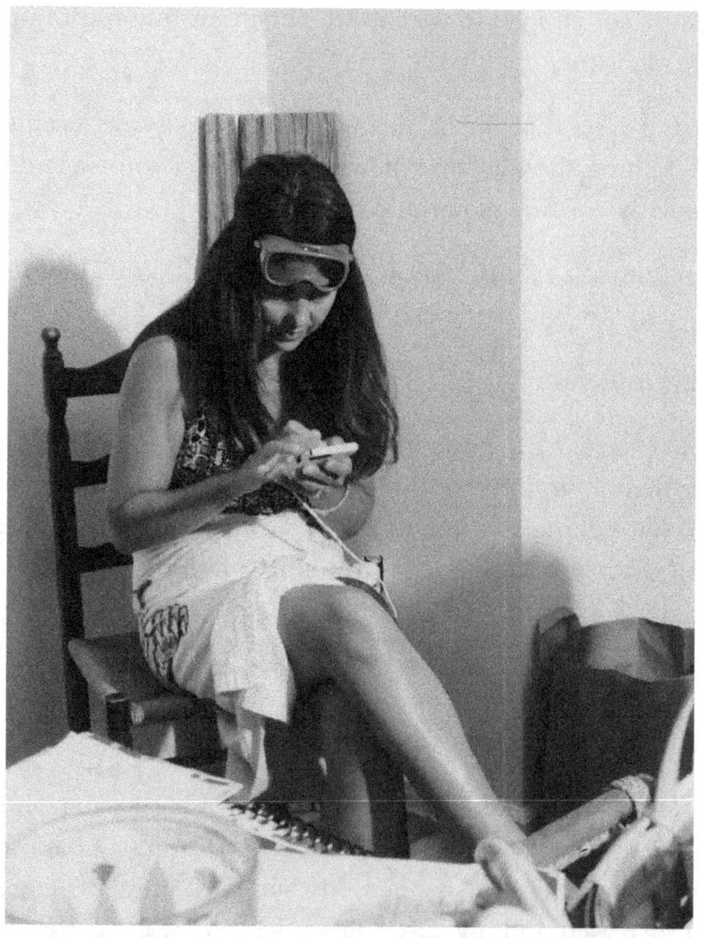

What an actual day of a top producer looks like ... playing with grandkids and closing out the year like a boss!

Not every day is glamorous, and sometimes you'll feel like you're putting in all this effort and seeing no return. But just know that your efforts are never in vain. Consistency is like planting seeds; it takes time, but eventually, it'll bloom.

The Framework to Build Your Online Presence

To create a powerful online presence, you need a strategy that keeps you focused. Here's how:

1. Define Your Brand Identity

- Start with you! What makes you stand out? What are your skills, passions, and values?

- Clarify your core message: What problem do you solve? What do you want to be known for?

- Position yourself as an authority by sharing valuable content—tutorials, tips, and insights.

- Maintain brand consistency across all platforms in your messaging, design, and tone.

2. Identify Your Unique Voice

- What do you stand for?

- What are you passionate about?

- What personal stories make your journey unique?

Authenticity is your greatest asset. People want to see the person behind the product. Share your journey, struggles, and wins—that's what makes you relatable.

3. Get Crystal Clear on Your Niche

- Who do you love serving the most? (Busy moms, entrepreneurs, fitness lovers?)

- What specific problems can you help solve?
- How can you position yourself as an expert in this space?

When you focus on a clear niche, your content speaks directly to the right people, making them feel understood.

4. Build Your Client Avatar

Create a mental image of your dream customer:

- Basic info: age, job, income, location.
- Pain points: What are their struggles? What keeps them up at night?
- Buying decisions: What motivates them to buy?
- Where do they hang out online? Facebook, Instagram, TikTok, YouTube?

5. Show Up Consistently

- Set a content schedule that works for you.
- Choose 1-2 platforms to focus on instead of trying to be everywhere.
- Commit to showing up, even when it feels like no one is watching.

6. Engage, Don't Just Broadcast

- Respond to comments and messages.
- Share stories and ask questions.
- Show behind-the-scenes moments to create connection.

The more you engage, the more your audience sees you as a real person, not just a salesperson.

7. Keep Refining Your Brand

Your brand will evolve as you grow. Stay in tune with what your audience needs and refine your message over time. Your client avatar should change as your business grows.

Trust Is Built in the Trenches

Every post, every live video, every moment you choose to show up adds up. Even if it feels like no one is watching, trust that your efforts are planting seeds that will grow into something bigger than you can imagine.

**"Do not despise these small beginnings, for
the LORD rejoices to see the work begin ..."**
Zechariah 4:10 (NLT)

How you show up online isn't just about posting links or sharing sales—it's about connection, trust, and building an authentic personal brand that attracts the right audience. When done right, your online presence becomes a magnet, and people are drawn to what you offer without you having to chase them.

People might buy from you once because they like the product, but they'll keep coming back when you consistently show up—because they trust *you*.

So don't wait for the perfect moment. The moment is now.

Show up. Be YOU. And build something that lasts.

Remember: **No one can be YOU better than YOU.**

Need more help? No more waiting! Grab my **365-day Social Media Content Calendar**, commit to showing up TODAY, and WIN BIG!

contentcalendar.susannormanonline.com

Key Takeaways to WIN

- **Trust is built through consistency**. Show up regularly and authentically to build trust with your audience.

- **You are the brand**. Focus on building your personal brand, not just promoting a product.

- **Narrow your focus**. Focus on a specific niche to attract the right audience and solve their problems.

- **Engage, don't just broadcast**. Connect with your audience by responding and sharing your story.

I Dare You to Take Action

I dare you to build your online presence.

You've learned how crucial it is to show up consistently, build trust, and position yourself as the go-to expert in your niche. Now, it's time to put that knowledge into action. I dare you to stop waiting for the "perfect" moment and start showing up today.

Ask yourself:

- Am I consistently showing up for my audience, or do I disappear when life gets busy?
- Does my online presence reflect my personal brand, or am I blending in with the crowd?
- Am I speaking to a clear niche, or am I trying to reach everyone (and connecting with no one)?

Here's your challenge:

Pick **one** area of your online presence to improve this week. Maybe it's committing to a weekly live video, defining your niche more clearly, or engaging more intentionally with your audience. Whatever it is—start now, tweak as you go, and keep showing up.

Success doesn't come from waiting—it comes from taking action. So, I dare you to show up, be yourself, and build something that lasts!

BE THE FREEBIE FAIRY & GROW YOUR EMAIL LIST!

*E*ver heard that saying, "*The money is in the list?*" Well, girl, it's true! If you're not working on growing your email list, you're missing out on one of the most powerful tools to help you scale your business.

I figured this out years ago when I realized my email list wasn't just a bunch of names—it was my future customers, my potential team members, and the key to real growth. So, I had to figure out *how* to start collecting those email addresses like my business depended on it, because honestly, it did.

That's when I learned all about using *lead magnets* and *landing pages* to capture emails.

Game. Changer. Suddenly, I had a system to bring people in, nurture them, and actually grow my business in a way that felt effortless. It was like unlocking a whole new world for my business!

Imagine walking into a party and being greeted by a friend who always brings the best snacks—you know the ones I'm talking about. They're so good you can't help but grab a second (or even third) helping because they're totally addicting.

Now, picture yourself being that friend, but instead of snacks, you're offering something even better—**freebies** that actually help.

Sprinkle a little fairy dust, and BOOM, you've got an audience that's hooked. When you offer value like that, you're not just giving away free stuff; you're building loyalty with your followers. It's like saying, "I'm here to help, and I've got something special just for you." And they won't forget it.

The Importance of Building Your Email List

Now listen, *social media followers don't actually equate to being your customer base*—they are simply your *audience*, and you need to move them from social media to a place where you can turn them into buying customers. That place is your **email list**. You see:

> **We use social media to grab people's attention and sell to them through our email list.**

When I partnered with a new direct sales company back in 2023, I knew firsthand that I had to capture emails to grow my business. My email list would become my leads! Those leads would become future customers and team members.

I literally had zero plans to go around prospecting using the old-school methods of "friend finding" or "warm chatting" every time I went out shopping or visiting friends and family. That's the worst! (Trust me, nobody likes that!) I wanted a faster, more effective way to grow my business, and it all came down to this: building my email list.

How Freebies Changed My Business

So, how does it work? Well, you start by asking yourself what your audience wants to learn about. In my case, it was a free guide with skincare tips, a recipe book, product samples, and easy makeup hacks.

When I created freebies to give away, I made sure I gave something that would speak to my specific audience. Stuff they really needed help with in exchange for one thing only—their EMAIL!

Once I had their email, I could build a relationship, start a conversation, and show them that I was there to help. The coolest thing behind all of this is that I didn't have to be online 24/7. Once someone signed up for my freebie, I could immediately send it to them through automations. No waiting, no manual follow-up needed.

Then a few days later, I'd follow up with another automated email like, "Hey, thanks for grabbing that free skincare guide! By the way, here are the exact products I use that make my routine a breeze. Check it out here."

It was a passive way to give them more of what they wanted without pushing too hard. And then, a few emails later, I'd share something like, "If you want to learn how to make extra income working from home like I do, click here." This would lead them to a recruiting funnel, where they could watch a video, learn about the opportunity, and potentially join my team.

What I loved the most about this process is that I didn't even have to be awake for it to work! I'd wake up in the morning to find a new team member had joined, all because of something I created and shared days or weeks before.

In my first two weeks, without prospecting or personally reaching out to a single person, I added 16 women to my front line. By the end of my first month, I had 25 people in my organization. Yep, you read that right—all through social media and the freebies I gave away. Granted, I had been showing up consistently online for some time to build an online presence, but adding freebies and focusing on building my email list made a big difference.

I even earned an all-expenses-paid trip to Mexico within my first few months, all from offering value and using freebies to grow my customer base. What made it feel so incredible was knowing I was helping people in a meaningful way.

Creating Your Own Irresistible Freebies

To create freebies that will grow your email list and attract the right people, you need to **know your audience**. Knowing exactly who you're speaking to, what they're interested in, and what would help them get results faster.

What you don't want to do is create something that your audience won't find valuable. It's like being a party host—would you serve food no one likes? Heck no! So think about what your audience is struggling with and create freebies that provide solutions.

For example, if you're a fitness coach targeting busy moms, a free seven-day meal plan with healthy recipes could be exactly what they need. Or if you're a beauty consultant, a skincare routine guide could be a perfect fit.

If you're not sure what to create, just ask! Run polls, ask questions in your stories, and engage with comments. Your followers will tell you what they need. Involving your audience is a win-win. They feel heard, and you get a better idea of what will truly connect with them.

These days, you don't need to be a design expert to create great freebies. You can find all kinds of free tools online, but here are two of my favorites:

- **Canva:** For creating stunning, professional-looking freebies, Canva is ideal. Even the free version works great! You can create everything from e-books and slide shows to quick checklists, and it's easy to use.

- **FlipHTML5:** If you're into creating digital flipbooks, this tool is perfect—and it's free! I use it to turn my PDFs into interactive flipbooks.

Once you play around with them, you'll see how easy it is to create beautifully designed freebies your audience will love.

Nail Your Opt-In Form and Landing Page

Once you've got your freebies created, you'll need an opt-in form and a landing page to capture those emails. Keep it simple—just ask for the essentials, like name and email. The easier you make it for people to sign up, the better. The more information you ask for, the higher the chance people will hesitate or skip the form altogether.

As for your landing page, make it look as inviting as possible. Use eye-catching images, bold headlines, and clear language that makes people say, "I *need* that!" Explain exactly what they will get in exchange for their email as simply as possible. Don't make them guess or wonder what they're signing up for.

Make sure your landing page looks good on mobile. People are browsing on their phones all the time, so you want to make sure it's easy to sign up no matter what device they're on.

You don't need to be a tech wizard to get this set up. There are plenty of budget-friendly services, such as Flodesk, Mailchimp, and Constant Contact, that make it pretty easy to create clean, simple opt-in forms and landing pages.

Promoting Your Freebies

Now that your landing page is set up to collect emails, it's time to promote your freebie and get the word out! Share them on social media, live events, reels, stories, or on your website (if you can). Make sure to promote them strategically, using catchy posts or videos that get people excited to sign up for your email list in exchange for the freebie.

If you're stuck on how to word it, tools like ChatGPT can help you write the perfect promo message. And don't forget the power of word-of-mouth. Ask your followers to share your freebies.

Nurturing Your Email List

Okay, you've grabbed the email addresses. Great! Now what? It's time to nurture your list. Think of it like keeping a conversation going with a friend. Send them helpful stuff like tips, tutorials, cool deals, or even video content that answers their questions. Make it feel personal. Use their names, and try to keep it real.

Don't overdo it with the promos, though. A little goes a long way! Balance is the key! People want to feel like you're there to help them, not just sell to them. Build that relationship, and when you do mention your products or services, it'll feel more like a friendly recommendation than a hard sell.

So, keep showing up and being genuine, and before you know it, your subscribers will be your biggest cheerleaders.

Key Takeaways to WIN

- **The money is in the list.** Building and nurturing your email list is key to long-term business growth.

- **Know your audience.** Get to know their pain points and desires to create content that resonates.

- **Freebies build trust.** Offering valuable freebies is a powerful way to attract and connect with your audience.

- **Keep it simple.** Your opt-in form and landing page should be clean, clear, and mobile-friendly for easy sign-ups.

- **Nurture, don't sell.** Email is for building relationships, not just pushing products. Give value first.

I Dare You to Take Action

I dare you to create your first freebie.

Girl, no more sitting on the sidelines watching others build thriving businesses while you hesitate. If you're not actively growing your email list, you're leaving money on the table—period.

So, I dare you. Yes, YOU. Right now. Take action:

1. **Create your freebie.** What's one thing your audience struggles with that you can help solve? Pick ONE idea and create a quick guide, checklist, or template. It doesn't have to be perfect—just valuable.

2. **Set up your opt-in page.** Don't overcomplicate it. Use a simple form with a headline that makes people say, "I need this in my life!" you can see how to do that here:

   landingpage.susannormanonline.com

3. **Start promoting TODAY.** Drop it in your social media bio, mention it in your stories, go live about it, or create a reel to tease what's inside. Don't be shy— let the world know what you're offering!

4. **Follow up with your list.** Send a welcome email as soon as they opt in. Keep it simple, warm, and engaging. Let them know what to expect from you!

Remember, success isn't about who has the best idea; it's about who takes ACTION. So no more waiting. No more overthinking. Go do it!

BOOKING TO WIN!

Starting a business can feel like putting together a 1,000-piece puzzle—overwhelming, confusing, and sometimes you don't even know where to start.

But here's what I found: there are three *BIG* things that you absolutely need to master if you want to see success in your business, especially in direct sales.

Booking. Selling. Recruiting.

That's it! Focus on those three things, and you'll see your business take off.

Over the next three chapters, we'll dive into each of these three things.

I'll be honest, I didn't have much time to figure this out, but I was determined to master them quickly. And here's why …

At the time, we were struggling. I had two little ones to take care of, we were living in low-income housing on WIC and Medicaid, and I didn't have a car. While Corbit was at one of his two jobs, I had to rely on my mom or my mother-in-law to get us around for appointments, grocery shopping … everything.

I needed to change our situation. Fast. The only way I was going to do that was by getting good at these three skills. I had no time to waste. Earning a car became my number one priority for my family and to lessen the burden on our parents. And guess what? I earned that car in my first 10 weeks in business.

But it wasn't easy. It wasn't like the car just magically appeared. I had to be willing to learn, get to work, and put in the effort every single day. I may have fumbled a little in the beginning, but I was determined to figure it out.

I had to push past my fears, my doubts, and my lack of experience. I became a student of the business, soaking up every bit of knowledge I could. I was willing to do whatever it took to succeed because I knew the stakes were high. I didn't wait for the "perfect time." I learned as I went, and over time, my skills improved.

It took me years to really get good at booking, selling, and recruiting. I didn't have all the answers at the start, but I kept going. And that's what I want you to know—don't wait for the perfect moment, don't wait until you have it all figured out.

The key is to keep learning, keep practicing, and keep moving forward. I'm sharing my best strategies with you now, so you don't have to waste the time I did figuring it out on your own.

Booking: Keep Your Calendar Full, Keep Your Business Growing

Booking appointments is your lifeline in direct sales. If you're not booking, you're not in business. It's the engine that keeps your business running. (And no one wants a blizzard in their datebook.) But it doesn't have to be complicated. The simpler you keep it, the better.

The Simple Booking Process

The first thing I want you to remember is this simple three-statement + one-question formula for every booking:

- "Here's what I'm doing." (Let them know what you're up to.)
- "Here's what I need." (Be clear about why you're asking them for help.)
- "Here's what's in it for you." (Make it worth their time.)
- "Are you with me?" (Close with a question to lock it down.)

For example:

> *"Hey Sally, it's Susan! You won't believe it, but I just started a new business, partnering with [insert company], and I could really use your help! I'm in a challenge right now to facial 30 faces in my first 30 days, and when I do, I'll earn [insert prize]. I just need practice, and I promise I won't hurt you (lol)! And just for helping me out, I'll have a $20 gift card for you. Any reason why you couldn't be one of my 30 and help me out?"*

That's it! You're offering value (the gift card), you're letting them know what you're doing (your challenge), and you're keeping it light and fun. They get to help you, and you're making it a win-win situation. Simple and effective.

The Power of Giving Choices

Now, when you're booking, don't just leave it at "When would be a good time?" Because they'll say three months from now! Give them options. People love options, plus it makes the process easier, and you need to take control of your calendar. For example:

> *"Okay great, so I have Thursday, April 10th, or Friday, April 11th. Which one works better for you?"*

Once they pick a day, offer another choice for the time:

> *"Awesome! Would 6:30 or 7:00 p.m. work better for you?"*

Once you settle on a time, you can use this pro tip and turn a booking into a party by saying:

> *"You know, Sally, if you'd like to have a few friends join you, I can do six faces just as easily as I can do one. And if you can, I will double your gift card and have a swag bag of goodies for your friends too! Any chance you might be able to include a few friends and help me get to my 30 faces faster?"*

If they say no, you really haven't lost anything, but if they say yes, you've just scored a huge victory!

Then, confirm the details:

> *"Okay, great! I'll see you Thursday, April 10th, at 7 p.m. I'll be there rain or shine! Please let me know 48 hours in advance if something comes up."*

See how easily I turned that booking into a party without asking her to book a party? This works great for any industry. Just tweak the wording to fit yours.

This simple technique makes it easy for your prospects to say "yes" because they feel in control, and you've made it so easy for them to commit.

But it doesn't stop there. To take it a step further and really grow your business, here's something that worked wonders for me once I got to the party to keep the bookings coming—and I'm excited to share it with you!

The Referral Game: Booking with Fun & Interaction

Every event or party, whether in person or virtual, is an opportunity to build your network and get more bookings. A great way to do that is by playing a referral game that gets everyone involved and thinking about who they know that could benefit from your products and services.

Here's how it works:

Step 1: Set the Scene and Get Them Involved

At every event or party, I always made sure to create a fun atmosphere. For example, I would act like a game show host, getting people instantly engaged and excited.

Closer to the end of the event (after all the demoing was done), I'd raise my hand and say,

"Who knows someone who is overworked and underappreciated?"

(It's psychological—if you raise your hand, they're more likely to follow suit.)

Then, I'd hand out a game sheet, which was just a cute piece of paper, to capture their referral information—this was pure gold. As they're writing, I'm either holding or standing next to a beautiful gift, something wrapped up and eye-catching, to get them excited about the prize.

Step 2: Introduce the Game and Set the Tone

Then, I'd say, *"Okay, it's game time! Who likes prizes?"* This always gets everyone pumped.

Next, I'd add a fun twist: *"Imagine you're on a deserted island, and your favorite Hollywood star is going to rescue you. You can only bring one of your favorite makeup items with you—lipstick, mascara, or eyeliner. Write it down!"* It's just a little fun to get them thinking.

Step 3: The Referral Part

After everyone's had their laughs and a little fun with the island scenario, I'd give them a specific task:

> *"Okay, now you have two minutes to write down all the women in your life who are overworked and underappreciated. And the person who writes down the most names and numbers will win the prize they wrote down earlier!"*

I'd start the timer and play some fun Jeopardy music on my phone from YouTube to keep things lively. At this point, I'd also joke around and say:

> *"You know, ladies, you can even cheat and use your phone! Oh, and extra points for those you write down who are over 25."*

Then I'd give them some suggestions while they were writing to jog their memory: Who are your …

- Neighbors
- Friends
- Family
- Hair stylists
- Nail techs
- Ladies at church

Step 4: Collect the Referrals

For in-person parties, when time was up, I'd say, *"Okay, pens down,"* and I'd have them count up their points and give a prize to the one with the most. Then I'd have everyone hand me their list.

For virtual parties, I gave them a clear deadline—usually about 30 minutes from the end of the live portion—to either DM me the list or text me a picture of it.

The interaction is key, and it keeps everyone engaged. If it was a virtual event, I would follow up with them personally by DMing them and by mailing out a small thank-you gift or gift card.

Once I got their lists, I'd start the whole booking process over again later that week by reaching out to those leads.

Booking Beyond Your Warm Market

When you're first starting out, booking appointments with people you know is an obvious place to start. But the real growth happens when you go beyond your warm market. And I just shared a great way to do that!

The key to making this happen? Simple. It's asking. Every time you finish an appointment, whether in person or virtual, ask the person you're with, "Who do you know who would enjoy 30 minutes of pampering?" Just ask!

There is a saying by Zig Ziglar that I've always loved, and it's this: "Timid salesmen have skinny kids." That holds true for asking for referrals and bookings to boot.

If I had allowed my fears of asking for bookings and referrals (*believe me, I had them*) to stop me when I was starting out, where would my family and I have been? Definitely without that car I worked so hard to earn, and probably relying on assistance way longer.

Instead, I made the decision to push through the fear, to ask for referrals, and to book beyond my warm market. That decision, that willingness to ask, changed everything for us.

The more appointments you have, the more opportunities you'll create. The more you do it, the better you'll get. Don't let fear hold you back. Asking for the appointment is the key to growing your business and, ultimately, changing your life.

Key Takeaways to WIN

- **Keep it simple**. Booking is the heartbeat of your business. Use a clear, confident ask: *Here's what I'm doing, here's what I need, and here's what's in it for you!*

- **Give choices, not open-ended questions**. Offer two date and time options to make it easy for them to say *yes*.

- **Turn one booking into more**. Use the *"bring a friend"* approach and referral games to keep your calendar full and your business growing.

- **Just ask!** Don't let fear hold you back. The more you ask, the more you book, and the faster your business will grow.

I Dare You to Take Action

I dare you to book.

You've just learned how to master booking to keep your calendar full and your business thriving. Now it's time to do it. Knowledge doesn't move the needle—action does. Stop overthinking. Ask for the appointment. Make booking a daily habit, not an occasional task.

Ask yourself:

- How many bookings do I need to hit my goals this month?
- Who are five people I can reach out to right now?
- How can I make my ask more confident and compelling?

Here's your challenge:

Today, reach out to five people using the simple booking process outlined in this chapter. Don't wait to feel ready. Momentum is built in motion.

Booking is the lifeline of your business. Every yes moves you forward, and every no gets you closer to the next yes. So take the leap, make the ask, and watch the momentum build. You've got this!

SELL TO WIN: TURNING CONVERSATIONS INTO SALES

Alright, now let's talk about selling. This doesn't mean being pushy or making people feel uncomfortable. It's about having natural conversations and leading them to see the value of what you offer. Selling is about finding a need and filling it. (Nowadays, people call it solving problems and offering value.)

Selling with Confidence

Confidence is key. If you believe in your products, that passion will come through in your conversations. When you're passionate about what you do, people want to be a part of it. Because, after all …

If you're afraid to sell it, they're afraid to buy it.

When you're selling, always lead with the *benefits*, not the *features*. Most people don't care about how many colors your product comes in or all the scientific micro ingredients. Some do, but most just want to know how it will improve their lives. So, focus on *how* your product can make their life better, easier, or more fun. That's what makes them want to buy.

Closing the Sale

There are two parts to a really good close in the world of Direct Sales. The group close (which is also called a "table close") and the individual close.

Let's start with the group close. This is when you use a closing sheet and help lead your clients through the sales process, sharing their options. This closing sheet is super powerful, and I'll explain why when we get to the individual close.

The Group Close

I'll use a personal example showing you how I would lead this, and you can make tweaks based on your industry …

So, we've done the facial, or the skincare party, and the referral game. Now it's time to close the sale. Here's how I would do it:

First, I'd say something like,

"Alright, ladies, I hope you had a great time! And I'd love to share with you the three ways you can get your products today as well as some specials too, so don't leave yet!"

Then, I'd walk through the three ways they can get their products: I'd say,

"Okay, so there are three ways you can get your products tonight!"

1. **"Become a Consultant.** Maybe you're looking to make some extra money or get your products at cost. Or maybe you saw something today that you loved and thought, *You know what? This isn't so hard. All she did was tell me to put this on and take it off! I can do that.* If that's

you, just put a little circle around that picture. Here's what you'd get if you decided to join us." (Then I'd explain the details of the kit, what they'll get for joining, and how much that costs.)

2. **"Book a Party.** Maybe you're thinking, This could be fun, I love free stuff, and I want to help Susie earn her hostess gifts. If that's the case, you can book a party (or whatever you call it in your company). And when you do, you get free stuff too! A reminder here: **You + 2 = a party.**" (I'd then go over how the hostess program works and share any current offers we have.)

3. **"Purchase Products.** Of course, if you're just here to shop, I've got some great specials you can take advantage of today."

I'd walk through all the products we tried, and then offer them three amazing options (tweak for your industry, of course) like these:

- **"The Queen of Everything Package.** This is the full package—cleanser, moisturizer, serum, everything we used today. If this is you, you'll get all these products for a special price today only." (Add a bonus, like a cute travel bag, for free.)

- **"The Princess Package.** Maybe you loved most of it, but don't need everything. This package is a great mid-range option." (I'd tell them the retail value and the special price.)

- **"The Basic Skin Care Set.** For those of you who just need the essentials—cleanser and moisturizer, this is a great option for you."

Then, I'd say, *"Okay, so, if money were no object, which of these options would you take home today?"*

Once they've had a moment to think, I'd go over the **Four-Question Close** with everyone as a group:

1. "If money were no object, which set would you choose: Queen of Everything, Princess Package, or Basic Skin Care?"

2. "At your second appointment, what would you like to learn more about—skincare, makeup, or body care?"

3. "Would you like your second appointment to be a private session, or would you prefer it to be a party so you can earn free stuff?"

4. "After everything you heard today, where do you see yourself partnering with us? Are you A, B, or C?

   A: Absolutely, sign me up today!

   B: Maybe, let's chat over coffee.

   C: I'll be a customer for now, and then we'll see."

Once they've answered those, I'd wrap up by saying:

> *"Alright, Suzy has some refreshments in the other room, so feel free to grab something. If anyone needs to leave first, let me know, but I'd like to meet with each of you individually to help with your order and answer any questions."*

And that's how I would close the sale as a group. But don't forget, the real magic happens when you meet with everyone individually to lock in the sale, book their second appointment, and potentially even recruit them.

The Individual Close

When it's time for the individual close, keep it simple with a few key questions that help uncover their needs:

- "Did you have a good time today?"
- "What was your favorite product that you tried (or learned about)?"
- "Do you have any questions or concerns we didn't cover?"
- "You know your current situation better than anyone else, and I noticed you selected 'Queen of Everything' if money were no object. Is that where you'd like to start?" (Tweak this to fit your industry.)

I remember one of the first times I asked that question. My client said, "Yes," and I responded, "You would?" (Definitely not the best answer!) I was so shocked that what I had been taught actually worked that I didn't know how to respond professionally. But hey, this approach works!

If they say "No," no worries—simply ask them:

"Where would you like to start today?"

It's all about keeping it flexible. Remember, at this stage, you already have their referral list. A close isn't complete without securing a second appointment or another booking. Because once the selling stops, the booking begins.

Once you've discussed their package and where they'd like to start, ask:

"So, when would be a good time for us to book your second appointment? Would this week or next be better?"

I assume they're ready for their second appointment because we've already talked about it during the table close. Now, after booking the second appointment, I transition into the party conversation. I might say something like:

"Hey, Sally, I noticed you have 10 names on your referral list here. Any chance you could get five or six of them together to earn free stuff and help Susie with her hostess gifts?"

This is where the magic of a good closing sheet comes in. Now, you hold the power. She can't say she doesn't know anyone because you've just shown her that she does. That's half the battle. Even if she says no, you still walk away with another booking and the chance to introduce her to more products. So, it's a win–win!

Lastly, I would look to see how they may have answered the question about teaming up. If they circled A, "absolutely sign me up," then I'd go ahead and ask them if they are ready to get started today with something like this:

You: *"I noticed that you circled A. You know, Sally, if we get you started now, we can always turn the party you just booked into your launch party. How does that sound?"*

If she says yes, I'd enroll her right on the spot.

If she was a "B" and might be interested, I'd say:

"I noticed you marked 'B,' indicating you're thinking about the opportunity but have some questions. I'd love to help clarify anything on your mind. Are there specific concerns or information you'd like more details on?"

If you're able to overcome any objections quickly and she's ready, sign her up. But if she mentions needing more time or wanting to consult with someone, acknowledge her need and propose a follow-up meeting by saying:

"I understand that you're interested but need a bit more time to think it over. How about we set up a time to grab coffee or have a quick call in the next few days? That way, I can answer any questions you might have and share more details to help you decide. What day works best for you, Tuesday [date] or Thursday [date]?"

By offering a specific follow-up meeting, you demonstrate your commitment to supporting their decision-making process without applying undue pressure.

Using a well-thought-out closing sheet and asking these questions gives you the insight you need to know about where your client stands and allows you to address any concerns before they become roadblocks.

Here's a sample of the kind of closing sheet I'd use:

Name_________________________ Ph# _____________

Address _______________________________________

City _______________ State_______ ZIP___________

Email ____

Birthday ______/______   Anniversary ______/______

The **Fabulous** Game

Gift your fabulous family & friends a relaxing Beauty Experience & gift certificate compliments of YOU! Simply write their name & number below.

1.________________ (___) ________ Text or Call
2.________________ (___) ________ Text or Call
3.________________ (___) ________ Text or Call
4.________________ (___) ________ Text or Call
5.________________ (___) ________ Text or Call
6.________________ (___) ________ Text or Call
7.________________ (___) ________ Text or Call
8.________________ (___) ________ Text or Call
9.________________ (___) ________ Text or Call
10.________________ (___) ________ Text or Call

Be a Brand Partner

◊ **Extra Money**
◊ **Flexibility—to be my own boss & work from home**
◊ **Fun & Girlfriend Time**
◊ **Prizes & Perks**
◊ **Self-Esteem & Confidence**
◊ **Tax Advantages**

BOOK a Party!

BUY FIRST TIME ORDERS GET AN ADDITIONAL 20% OFF!

Queen of Everything

PLUS GET A FREE TRAVEL BAG!

Princess Package

Basic Skincare

Tell me what you think...

1. If money were no object which set would you choose?

____ Queen of Everything

____ Princess Package

____ Basic Skin Care

2. At your 2nd appointment what would you like to learn more about? ___Skin Care ___Make-up ___Body Care

3. Would you like it to be:

___ Private sesh ___Party & get FREE stuff

4. After everything you heard today where would you see yourself partnering with me?

____A– absolutely, sign me up now!

____B– I might be, buy me coffee and let's chat more.

____C- I'll be a customer for now and then we'll see.

Key Takeaways to WIN

- **Selling = solving problems**. Keep it simple. Find a need, share how your product helps, and focus on benefits, not features.

- **Confidence sells**. If you believe in it, they will too! Your passion is your best sales tool.

- **Close with a system**. Use a closing sheet to guide the group, then seal the deal one-on-one.

- **Always book the next step**. A sale, a party, or a follow-up—never leave without a next step!

I Dare You to Take Action

I dare you to sell with confidence.

Selling isn't about pushing products, it's about serving people. You've just learned how to guide conversations naturally, highlight value over features, and close with confidence. Now, it's time to take action.

Ask yourself:

- Am I holding back from selling because of fear or self-doubt?
- How can I shift my mindset to see selling as helping, not pressuring?
- Do I have a structured approach to closing the sale, or am I winging it?

Here's your challenge:

The next time you present your products, use the structured closing process. Walk your customers through their options, ask the right questions, and confidently guide them toward a decision.

Don't wait until you feel 100% ready because confidence comes from action, not the other way around. The more you practice, the better you'll get.

RECRUITING: BUILDING YOUR WINNING TEAM

I learned early on that recruiting was the best way to duplicate my time and make more money faster. I understood that I couldn't be everywhere at one time, but if I had a team of 50 or 100, let's say, we could all be holding appointments at the same time, which meant we were selling way more than I could on my own. That just made sense to me and seemed way more sustainable.

Honestly, if you want to make really good money with your home business, you'll want to recruit, and not just anyone, but the right people who are excited about the opportunity to grow with you.

Who Are You Looking For? Know the "Types"

Over the years, I learned to choose at least two recruit leads from every party I did. And, although you never want to pre-judge anyone, these were the four types of customers that I always looked for first:

- **Chatty Kathy.** She's the one who loves to talk and connect with others. She's great at building relationships, and she's usually a great person to have on your team.

- **The person who bought the most.** Clearly, she loves the products and may enjoy getting them at a discount.

- **The person who bought the least.** She may need the extra money, so don't discount her.

- **The Shiny Penny:** This is the person who just stands out to you for some reason, whether she's super excited (one you have to reel in) or the quiet one who didn't say much. (I was that girl!) Don't let her quietness fool you. These are often the ones who surprise you the most. With a little nurturing, they can become rock stars once they're on board.

How to Do a Recruiting Appointment

Using the **APPS** method is super easy to remember whenever you are doing an in person event, Zoom, or live call when it comes to a recruiting opportunity. APPS stands for Acquaint, Purpose, Pain, Solution.

1. **Acquaint: Building a Personal Connection**

   Begin with a warm greeting to establish rapport.

   You: "Hey Sally, It's Susan! I'm excited to chat with you today. How's your day going so far?"

   (Pause and listen attentively to her response.)

   You: "I've heard such wonderful things about you from [Referrer's Name]. They mentioned you might be curious about joining our team, and I'd love to share more. But first, tell me a bit about yourself—how's your family? Do you have kids? What do you do for work?" [Allow them to share, showing genuine interest and noting details to connect on.]

You: "That sounds like a full and rewarding life! Many women I speak with juggle family, work, and personal time. That's actually one of the reasons I love what I do—it offers flexibility and fits around my life."

2. Purpose: Setting the Stage

Set the intent for the conversation.

You: "Here's what I'd love for us to do today: I'll share a bit about my journey, explain the opportunity, and answer any questions you might have. No pressure at all. Whether this turns out to be the right fit for you or not, you might know someone who might be interested. And it doesn't cost a dime to look or listen. Does that sound good?"

"Okay, great."

Share your personal "I" story. (Focus on why you got started, how long ago, a few successes, and what you love about your journey with the company.)

For example:

You: "When I first started, I was just looking for a way to make a little extra money for my family—I had no sales experience, no business background, and honestly, I was pretty shy. But I quickly realized that this business was more than just extra income—it gave me confidence, friendships, and the flexibility to work around my life, not the other way around.

"In my first few months, I earned [mention a specific achievement—like first paycheck, first customer, or first team member], and that showed me what was possible.

Now, I get to help other women do the same, and it's incredibly rewarding!"

3. Pain—Understanding Her Needs

Explore Their Motivations: Ask open-ended questions to uncover her motivations and challenges, and most importantly, her *"WHY."*

You: "Let me ask you—if you could change one thing about your current situation—maybe it's having more flexibility, earning extra income, or just having something fun for yourself, what would it be?"

(Listen carefully to their response.)

You: "How would achieving that change things for you and your family?

(Let her answer—this is GOLD! Her response will tell you exactly how to position your opportunity to meet her needs.)

You: "So what I heard you say was that you're looking for (summarize their main points and repeat it back). Is that right? I totally get that."

4. Solution:

Presenting the Business Opportunity

You: That's exactly what our team is all about—helping women like you build a business from home to create income and flexibility without sacrificing what matters most. Plus, you don't need any sales experience— we provide all the training and support you need! The best part? You can start part-time, work around your schedule, and grow it at your own pace! Let me quickly share how it works!"

Highlight Key Benefits Using the MRS CAB Framework:

○ **Money**. "Our compensation plan is straightforward and rewarding, allowing you to earn based on your efforts." (Quickly share the streams of income.)

○ **Recognition**. "We celebrate achievements with incentives, awards, and trips, creating a supportive community."

○ **Self Confidence**. "Personal growth is a big part of this journey; many women find they become more confident and empowered."

○ **Cars.** "Some of our top achievers have earned car bonuses, adding an extra perk to their success."

○ **Advancement.** "Grow your business at your own pace. Get promoted when you do the work."

○ **Be your own boss.** "Running your own business offers significant advantages, including the freedom to set your own schedule and potential tax benefits. This flexibility allows you to prioritize family, pursue personal passions, and work toward your financial goals on your terms."

5. **The Five Question Close: Guiding Their Decision**

You: "Based on what we've discussed, I'd love to hear your thoughts."

1. "What did you like most about what you just heard?"

2. "If you were to ever consider doing this, would you want to make a little or a lot?" "What for?"

3. "If everything stayed exactly as it is today with your current situation, how long would it take to reach those goals?"

4. "Are you okay with that?"

Present Enrollment Options, What Comes with the Kit, and How Much It Costs:

5. "From everything we've talked about, where do you see yourself?"

   A. "Absolutely! I'm ready to start!"

   B. "I may be, but I have a few more questions."

   C. "I'd like to be a customer for now and see how it goes."

6. **Next Steps Based on Their Response**

   If They Choose A (Ready to Start):

   o **You**: "That's fantastic! I'm so excited for you. Let's get you enrolled and set up. I'll send you the link right now, and we can go through the process together."

(Guide them through the enrollment process, ensuring they feel supported.)

Don't wait—get them signed up immediately and make it official. Stay on the phone with them to do this, or if you are with them in person, help them on the spot.

If They Choose B (Interested but Have Questions):

- **You**: "I love that you're thinking it through—that tells me you're serious. Let me ask you: What's the one thing holding you back from saying yes today? Or what would you need to know to feel 100% confident moving forward?"

(Pause, listen carefully, and let her share.)

Address each question or concern honestly and simply—don't overwhelm her with too much information. You're not convincing, you're *guiding*.

If she's still unsure, that's totally okay. You can say:

- **You**: "How about we schedule a quick coffee chat or phone call to go over everything together? I want to make sure you feel completely confident either way to discuss this further."

Then suggest a specific day and time:

- **You**: "Would [insert date/time] work for you?"

(Confirm the meeting details and express your enthusiasm to connect again.)

If she's leaning in and you sense she's ready but needs a little nudge, gently guide her:

- **You**: "You know, it sounds like you're almost there. Want to go ahead and get you started while it's fresh and exciting?"

If They Choose C (Customer for Now):

- **You**: "That's a great start. Many begin as customers and later decide to join the business side. Let's set you up with our products/services, and we can revisit the opportunity whenever you're ready."

(Ensure they have all the information they need to get started as a customer.)

Pro Tips When Recruiting:

- **Be enthusiastic but natural**—energy attracts!
- **Ask open-ended questions** to get her talking.
- **Listen for her needs** and tailor your response.
- **Simplify the opportunity**—don't overwhelm with details.
- **Set a next step** to keep momentum going.

The Steps for Success

The bottom line is that booking, selling, and recruiting are the three keys to making money in direct sales. They don't have to be complicated or overwhelming. Break them down into simple, actionable steps, and stay consistent.

Focus on booking that first appointment. Ask those questions to close the sale. Find the right recruits. The more you do it, the better you'll get. And before you know it, you'll have a thriving, profitable business.

Key Takeaways to WIN

- **Recruit to grow**. Building a team lets you work smarter, not harder. More people means more sales and less stress for you.

- **Find the right fit**. Look for people who love the products, need extra income, or have that spark—these are your future rock stars.

- **Use the APPS method**. Keep it simple—connect, share your story, understand their needs, and offer the solution.

I Dare You to Take Action

I dare you to recruit one person this week.

Recruiting may feel intimidating at first, but it's the key that frees up your time and accelerates your income. If you've been hesitant, I challenge you to take the leap right now.

It doesn't have to be perfect—just genuine. Think about the people you've connected with recently and choose one person to approach about joining your team.

Here's your action plan to use what you learned in this chapter and take the steps:

- Identify the lead.
- Reach out to schedule the appointment.
- Present the opportunity using the APPS Method.
- Close within 24 to 48 hours.
- Guide them through enrollment so they feel supported from the start.

Remember, every person you recruit has the potential to shift your entire business, but it starts with that first step. So I dare you: go recruit that one person. It might be the game changer you've been waiting for.

Take action now and watch your business grow.

MEMORIZE IT LIKE YOU MEAN IT

Growing up, my oldest daughter, Kaela, was part of something called Bible Quiz. If you've never heard of it, think of it like *Jeopardy* for Christian teens—except instead of random trivia, these kids memorize entire chapters, and even full books of the Bible, and then get quizzed on them.

Yeah. Word for word. Verse by verse. Not paraphrased. *Memorized.*

Each year, they'd focus on a different book of the Bible. We're talking about in-depth scripture, studied and practiced for hours on end. Kaela would commit whole passages to memory, able to tell you the exact verse if you called out the chapter. That kind of dedication? It didn't just happen by chance. It took time. Discipline. Passion.

The Power of Being All In

I remember one year when she was around 16 or 17, her team even made it all the way to the national championships.

But you know what stuck with me that I admired the most, more than the trophies they got?

The hours she put in behind the scenes. Quietly. Consistently. Intentionally.

Because champions are made long before the stage lights come on.

> **"Everyone who competes in the games
> goes into strict training. They do it to get
> a crown that will not last, but we do it to get
> a crown that will last forever."**
> 1 Corinthians 9:25 (NIV)

Now Let's Talk About You

That kind of dedication made me think about this industry— direct sales, network marketing, entrepreneurship. So let me ask you:

How well do *you* know your business?

Could you quote your compensation plan like Kaela quoted scripture?

Could you confidently explain the benefits of your top three products to a stranger at a coffee shop?

Do you know the next rank you're aiming for and *exactly* what it takes to get there?

I can't tell you how many times I've been on coaching calls and asked,

> "So, what's your next goal?"
> "What's the payout for that promotion?"
> "How does your company structure bonuses?"

And I kid you not—a lot of the time—I'll hear:

"I'm not sure …"
"I haven't looked at that yet …"
"I just kind of wing it."

Friend, let me shoot straight with you—*you are leaving money on the table.*

If your company is offering it, you should *know it*—inside and out.

Winning Requires More Than Dabbling

Kaela didn't memorize the Bible because it was easy. She did it because she was committed. Because she knew what was at stake. Because she wanted to win.

It's no different for you. If you want to grow a business that provides real freedom, real income, and real impact, you've got to be obsessed with the details.

Learn your products.

Master your compensation plan.

Know your scripts so well you can say them in your sleep.

Get so good at handling objections and closing conversations that it feels like second nature.

You don't get great at something by dabbling. You get great by going all in.

You're in the Championship, Too

Listen, your journey might not come with a trophy at the end—but that doesn't mean it's not a championship.

You're running your own race. You're building a business that could change your life and your family's legacy.

So don't just "kinda sorta" know your stuff.

Become the expert. Own your business. Memorize it like you mean it.

Key Takeaways to WIN

- **Success rewards the prepared.** Winging it won't win. Knowing your business inside and out *will*.

- **Commitment beats talent every day of the week.** Give me someone who's committed and they can be turned into a rock star. I was never the smartest one in the room, but I can guarantee I was willing to work the hardest.

- **Study your business like it's your Bible quiz.** Master your scripts, your products, and your plan. Champions study.

- **Go all in. No more dabbling.** If you want next-level results, give next-level effort.

I Dare You to Take Action

I dare you to memorize it like you mean it!

- **Choose one area of your business to master this week.** Is it your product line? Your compensation plan? Your closing skills? Pick one.

- **Create a "know-it-cold" list.** These are the top five things you need to know like the back of your hand. Write them down. Practice them. Own them.

- **Practice out loud.** Don't just study in your head, say it out loud. Role play. Rehearse. Sharpen your skills until they're second nature.

COMMUNICATING FOR SUCCESS: THE POWER OF DISC

I used to think I was great at communicating ... until my business (and my bank account) proved otherwise.

When I look back at my business journey, I'll admit that I wasn't always the communication pro that I am today.

When I started my first direct sales business all those years ago, booking appointments, closing sales, and recruiting new team members felt like an uphill battle. I'd get on the phone, all fired up, ready to seal the deal, only to have the conversation fizzle out faster than they could say, "No thank you."

And recruiting? Don't even get me started. I'd get all excited about the opportunity, thinking I had the perfect pitch, only to get crickets on the other end most of the time.

I remember one time trying to close a sale with a client who was just not biting. I was giving all the details, showing her the benefits, laying out the whole shebang.

But she just kept nodding politely and saying, "Hmm, okay ..." and I knew I wasn't getting anywhere. It was like trying to sell someone a fur coat in the middle of a heatwave—needless to say, it didn't go well.

The worst part? I had no idea why. So, there I was, thinking, "What the heck am I doing wrong?"

The real problem? I didn't understand people's personalities, or how much that mattered for booking, selling, and recruiting. I had no idea that people process information differently, or that some needed all the details while others just want the big picture. I kept trying to mold everyone into the same style and, surprise, surprise—it wasn't working.

The Breakthrough

Then I discovered something that changed everything: DISC Personality training.

It was like someone finally turned on the lights, and things started clicking for me. And I mean really clicking.

I finally understood that my approach needed to change depending on who I was talking to. You know, there's this saying, "You can't fit a square peg into a round hole." Well, in sales, I was trying to fit every conversation into the same box—and let me tell you, that never works.

When I got my hands on the DISC personality tool, I felt like I'd been handed the secret decoder ring to communication. Truth is, each personality type needs to be communicated with differently. Once I cracked the code, the results spoke for themselves.

I went from stumbling through conversations, struggling to close deals and feeling frustrated, to confidently booking appointments, closing sales, and even recruiting people who were actually excited to join my team. And guess what? It made me a better mom, wife, and friend, too.

I'll give you a perfect example: I used to get so frustrated when a friend or family member did things that seemed to annoy or irritate me. I'd think, "Why are you doing this to me?!" But after learning DISC, I finally understood it wasn't about me. It was about the way their brain was wired.

When I started to view their actions through their mind's eye, I realized it wasn't personal. They weren't trying to bug me, hurt me, or make me mad; (usually), they just processed the world differently. This shift helped me in every relationship, not just in business.

So, here's the breakdown: DISC gave me a fresh perspective. Once I began to communicate based on someone else's personality type, not only did I get better results with my business, but I also got better results at home with my family and friends.

What Is DISC?

Think of DISC as your secret communication superpower.

It stands for Dominance, Influence, Steadiness, and Conscientiousness, and once I got the hang of it, everything in my business (and my life!) started clicking into place. Instead of guessing what my clients or team members needed, I could recognize their personalities and adjust how I communicated with them.

Not everyone communicates or makes decisions the same way. Some people want the bullet points and bottom line. Others need stories, connection, and time to process. Once you get that, you can stop spinning your wheels and start building real momentum.

Now don't worry, I'm not about to throw a textbook at you. This isn't about memorizing a bunch of psychology terms. It's about noticing patterns, tuning in to people, and learning how to connect in a way that actually gets through.

Let me give you a quick taste of each style …

- **D** personalities are direct, driven, determined, and decisive. They don't need fluff—they need results. You want to get to the point and show them the outcome.
- **I** personalities are the life of the party. They are inspirational, influencing, impressive, and interactive. Think fun, fast-talking, and full of energy. With them, you want to keep things upbeat and engaging.
- **S** personalities are steady, supportive, sentimental, and super loyal. They value trust and connection over speed. Take your time, be warm, and show them you care.
- **C** personalities are careful, conscientious, competent, and critical. They don't just want answers, they want detailed answers. Be prepared, be precise, and don't rush them.

Every person you meet, whether it's a customer, a teammate, a friend, or your spouse, has a style that influences how they hear you, how they trust you, and how they decide. When you learn how to spot it, speak to it, and honor it, you'll walk into every conversation with confidence, knowing exactly how to connect with whoever is in front of you.

Proof in Action (the Elevator Story)

Let me give you a real-life example.

It was my company's annual seminar, and we were staying at this *massive* hotel. It was like 30 stories tall. It even had a rooftop pool, which is where our team was meeting that night for a pizza party, desserts, and a little celebration.

Right before I headed up, I got a message from one of my leaders asking if I could bring an ice bucket with me. Easy enough. I'd seen one in my hotel room, so I grabbed it and made my way to the elevator.

Now listen, this elevator? It moved *fast*. The kind that shoots straight up like a rocket and makes your stomach do backflips. I already didn't love getting on it, but I figured I'd survive one more ride.

So I stepped in with two other women, hit the rooftop button, and up we went … until we didn't.

With no warning, the elevator jolted. Then stopped. Midway between floors. We looked at each other like, "That's weird," thinking maybe it was just a quick pause. But nope. We were stuck.

We started pressing buttons, trying to figure out what to do. Eventually, we found the emergency call button, but we didn't even know what floor we were on. Turns out, we were between them. So we waited. And waited.

It started getting hot in there. No air circulation. Tension building. And that's when panic started to set in.

Now, I don't know about you, but getting stuck in a small box suspended between floors is not exactly where I thrive. I could feel the anxiety creeping up. But the woman next to me? She was already freaking out. Pushing all the buttons, talking fast, and clearly anxious.

Even though I was totally panicking on the inside (I mean, my brain already had us plummeting to our doom), I knew I had a choice: match her energy or manage mine.

I stayed calm, took a deep breath, and steadied my voice. I wanted her to feel safe, so I said something like, "Hey, I know this isn't ideal, but we're okay. Help's on the way!

Just like that, she calmed down. The whole atmosphere shifted.

That's the power of communication. And without realizing it, I was leaning on what I'd learned years earlier with DISC.

My calm words gave her what she needed to feel safe. That's what DISC does—it helps you connect in a way that builds trust, no matter the situation.

Eventually, the crew got us out (yes, I was still holding the bucket). And when I got to the rooftop, my leader smiled and said, "Susan! Did you bring the ice?" I just shook my head. "Wait … you wanted ice?! I thought you meant the bucket!"

That experience taught me something important—**how you communicate can either calm the storm or stir it up**—even in life's elevator moments.

The Goal Is Connection

DISC completely changed how I interact with people. Understanding different personality styles helped me communicate effectively, close more sales, and build a stronger team. The breakthrough came when I learned to adjust my communication style to match others.

Mastering DISC isn't about changing yourself. It's recognizing that everyone has different needs and adapting your approach. This isn't just theory; it's a tool that has driven massive growth in my business.

Seriously … booking? Easier. Selling? More natural. Recruiting? Way more effective. And relationships? Whew. So much more grace and understanding.

I go into all of this (and how to apply it like a rock star) in my full DISC course. But for now, just know this: the key to better communication isn't saying *more*—it's saying it in a way that actually connects. And that, my friend, is the magic of DISC.

Want to master this and turn conversations into conversions?

Let's go deeper.

Check out my full Powerful Persuasion DISC course where I'll walk you through how to use these styles to book, sell, and recruit with more ease and confidence than ever before.

Trust me—you're gonna wish you'd had this sooner.

powerfulpersuasion.susannormanonline.com

You've Got What It Takes to Rock This

No matter where you are on your journey—just starting out or getting back on track—remember this: you *can* book, sell, and recruit like a rock star. It's not about knowing it all right away. It's about showing up, taking the next step, and building your business one win at a time.

Key Takeaways to WIN

Even if you don't dive into the course just yet, here's one way to start using DISC right away:

Talk to your people the way *they* want to be talked to.

- **Fast talker** and straight to the point? Probably a High D. Get to the results quickly.

- **Super bubbly** and full of stories? Hello, High I. Bring the fun and excitement!

- **Warm and steady**? That's your loyal High S. Build trust and be consistent.

- **Detail-oriented** and loves facts? High C. Be thorough and clear.

It doesn't have to be complicated. Start by noticing how people show up, and meet them where they are. Understanding personalities helps you connect faster, serve better, and sell smarter.

I Dare You to Take Action

I dare you to become a better communicator.

Now that you know the power of DISC, it's time to put it into practice!

1. **Have you identified your DISC personality type?** D, I, S, or C?

2. **Identify three people.** Think of three people in your life (clients, team members, or even family) and determine their DISC personality type.

3. **Adapt Your Approach.** In your next conversation, adjust your communication style based on what you've learned. Be direct with a "D," bring energy with an "I," show support with an "S," and provide details for a "C."

4. **Take the Next Step!** Want to master this skill even faster? Grab your FREE **Persuasion Quick Start** guide to help you quickly identify personality types and learn how to communicate with them effectively.

Download it here:

discguide.susannormanonline.com

PROGRESS OVER PERFECTION

Raise of hands. Where are all my perfectionist friends? If you're the type who wants everything *just right* before taking action, I see you. I *am* you. Well, at least, I *was* you.

You see, I'm a recovering perfectionist.

In the early days of my direct sales career, I wanted to do everything just right. I wanted to read every piece of literature, watch all the training videos, and make sure I understood the ins and outs. I wanted to come across as knowledgeable, prepared, and professional.

But, as you know, our financial situation was dire, and I had no time to waste. I couldn't afford to sit on the sidelines and wait until I felt 100% ready. We had bills to pay, and I knew that if I wanted to make money, I had to take action—and take action *fast*!

For me, the challenge wasn't starting, it was learning how to be flexible when things didn't go according to plan. And, oh, did I learn that lesson fast!

The Best Laid Plans

I remember an early party I organized with a mix of great excitement and nervous energy, ready to take on the world. A family member had promised to invite some women to help, and I was *thrilled*. Finally, a little victory!

But my excitement was short-lived. When I arrived at the house, my heart sank. The room was nearly empty. Just the hostess and one guest. The space felt too quiet, and my stomach twisted as I realized the turnout wasn't what I'd expected.

I'd always heard that "you plus two makes a party," but this was supposed to be the hostess *plus* two—leaving me feeling a bit lost in the sea of empty chairs.

I felt a bit deflated, and despite the initial disappointment, I took a deep breath, planted my heels firmly against the floor, and reminded myself, *I am here to do my best, no matter who's watching.*

Then, as if by some miracle, one more person arrived. *Woohoo!* Things were looking up.

The first name of that guest has since faded from memory, but I'll never forget her last name. And you'll understand why in just a moment.

Okay, I was ready to start. First on the outline: introductions. Easy enough. Share my story, check. Thank the hostess, check. Now, let's have the guests share their names and how they know the hostess.

And that's when things took a peculiar turn.

One of the guests, the one with the unforgettable last name, shared her first name and then stood up, and suddenly, without warning, burst into song.

"Chestnuts roasting on an open fire …"

I froze, like a deer caught in the headlights. Standing there with an awkward smile on my face, trying to figure out what to do or say next, I could feel my brain processing. But my face? Well, my face said it all without my permission.

I'm pretty sure I looked like I'd just bitten into a lemon—complete with that confused, slightly horrified expression that I'm certain I didn't hide as well as I had hoped.

I sat there thinking, *What is happening right now?* And then it hit me. *Ohhhhhhh, her last name is Chestnut.* It was like her life was a musical, and she was the STAR!

Somehow, I managed to pull myself together, letting out a nervous little laugh, and said something like, "Well, thank you for introducing yourself … so creatively." Honestly, it was the best I could come up with in that moment as I tried to steer the conversation back on track.

As the afternoon continued, Mrs. Chestnut kept bursting into song every few minutes, her voice filling the space between my words as I fumbled through my presentation. Every time I thought I had found my rhythm—bam! Another unexpected verse.

At one point, I thought, *There is no way I'm going to get through this.* But somehow, I did. And just when I thought I'd completely lost control of the event, Mrs. Chestnut did something that left me speechless.

She placed a HUGE order—pretty much everything I had just demoed.

I couldn't believe it!

I learned something valuable that day. People don't show up for perfection. They show up for connection. They just want to feel seen, heard, and, honestly, have a little fun.

I realized my job wasn't to be flawless, it was to make people feel comfortable, create an experience, and offer real solutions. That day, I stopped stressing over everything going perfectly according to plan. Instead, I learned to roll with the unexpected, laugh at the awkward moments, and focus on the people in front of me.

Taking Imperfect Actions Beats Standing Still

Now, how might this look in your business? Progress over perfection shows up in so many ways:

- **Hosting your first event:** You might not have the perfect setup, the biggest crowd, or the best sales pitch—but showing up and giving it your best is what matters.

- **Making that first call:** You might stumble over your words or forget what you were going to say, but taking action is what moves the needle.

- **Going live on social media:** You might feel awkward, your lighting might be off, or you might trip over your words. But people don't expect perfection—they want authenticity.

- **Following up:** You may not have the perfect words scripted, but a simple "Hey, just wanted to check in" is better than waiting for the right thing to say.

Embrace Messy Moments

In direct sales, perfection is a myth. If you're waiting for the perfect moment, the perfect event, or the perfect version of yourself to start showing up and taking action—stop. The real growth happens when you embrace the messy moments, adjust as you go, and stay focused on serving others.

Think about your own journey. Where have you been holding back because things weren't *just right*? Where have you been waiting instead of acting? What would happen if you took imperfect action today?

The magic happens when you embrace the imperfections, laugh through the awkward moments, and keep moving forward anyway.

In the end, progress will always matter more than perfection.

Key Takeaways to WIN

- **Start before you're ready.** If you wait for the perfect circumstances, you'll never get started. Success comes from showing up and taking action, even when things aren't ideal.

- **Done is better than perfect.** People don't remember flawless execution; they remember how you made them feel. Aim for progress, not perfection.

- **Adapt and adjust.** Plans will change, and unexpected moments will happen. Growth comes from learning to adjust, not from having everything go perfectly.

- **Connection over perfection.** People resonate with realness. Your imperfections make you relatable, and your willingness to roll with the punches builds trust.

- **Laugh through the chaos.** Not everything will go smoothly, and that's okay. The ability to laugh through the awkward moments makes the journey more enjoyable.

I Dare You to Take Action

I dare you to embrace imperfection.

You've read all about how perfection can hold you back and how taking imperfect action is often the key to progress. Now, it's time to stop waiting for everything to be *just right*. I dare you to start taking action *now*, even if things aren't perfect.

Here's your challenge:

1. **Choose one area you've been overthinking.** You know the one—it's been sitting on your to-do list because you're waiting to feel "ready."
2. **Commit to taking action within 24 hours.** No more stalling. Send the message. Schedule the event. Hit the "Go Live" button. Just do it.
3. **Embrace the mess.** When it feels awkward or goes sideways (because it might), smile, laugh, and keep going. That's progress.
4. **Celebrate the win.** Not the perfect result—the fact that you took action. That's what separates dreamers from doers.

Remember, people don't need you to be flawless—they need you to be *real*. You're not building a business based on perfection. You're building it on courage, connection, and consistent, imperfect steps forward.

So … I dare you.

This week, stop waiting. Start doing.

Take one bold, imperfect step. Watch how far it takes you.

YOUR FOCUS CREATES YOUR FUTURE

There was a season in my life when it felt like everything that could go wrong, did. When life just throws a ton of punches at you all at once, leaving you standing there thinking, "Seriously?"

It started with the loss of sweet Taby. And just when I thought I couldn't take more bad news, I was told I would have to step down from my position as sales director. As you know, this wasn't just any position—it was a role I had worked so hard for and poured my heart into. The news hit me like a ton of bricks.

And still, despite the setbacks, I chose to show up for the leadership conference that I had already paid for. I was no longer part of the leadership team, so I had to get special permission to attend, but I knew my vision was bigger than my current circumstances.

Have you ever felt like you were being tested? Like God was asking, "How badly do you want this?" That's exactly where I found myself.

Seeing It Before You See It

Early on in my journey, I quickly realized how important it was to have a clear vision of where I was headed. That's when I adopted the phrase, "You've got to see it, before you see it, in order to see it." Which basically means, you've got to have a clear picture in your mind of what you want before you can make it happen.

And that's where faith comes in. Scripture says that if you have faith the size of a mustard seed, you can move mountains (Matthew 17:20).

So even if your vision feels small at first—like just a tiny seed—when you hold it with faith and keep it in front of you, it grows. That little seed of belief is enough to start creating momentum toward the life and business you're praying for.

Even when I lost my director position, that vision remained crystal clear in my mind. I could still see where I was going, even when the path got rocky. That clarity was what pushed me to attend the leadership conference despite everything working against me.

When you have a vivid picture of your destination—whether it's building a successful business, creating a legacy for your family, or making an impact in your community—it becomes an anchor that holds you steady during life's storms.

Why Your Vision Matters More Than You Think

This vision is like a roadmap for your business. It helps you stay focused on the bigger picture, so when things get crazy or you feel stuck, you can remind yourself why you started. Without that, it's easy to get caught up in the daily hustle and forget where you're going.

To get there, it starts with looking inward. Take some time to ask yourself what you really want and why. It should be rooted in your values, passions, and purpose.

When your vision aligns with your deepest values, it becomes more than just a goal—it becomes a calling. That's when you find the strength to push through hardships, like I did when I showed up to that conference despite everything telling me to just stay home.

A clear vision gives you:

- Direction when you feel lost
- Motivation when you feel defeated
- Clarity when everything seems chaotic
- Purpose when tasks feel meaningless

What's your vision? Can you see it clearly? If not, it might be time to revisit it.

What You Focus on Gets Bigger

It was my first trip ever to Hollywood, and I was so excited to do all the things—walk the boulevard, go to all the parties, and enjoy some fun time with my girlfriends.

But nope! I got the flu. And not just any flu—the kind that leaves you shaking with fever and chills for days. I had already gone through a difficult few months, and now this.

Let me paint the picture for you …

I got to Hollywood, and of course, my suitcase got mixed up with someone else's. I didn't get to my hotel until midnight. Then I had to wait for another hour or two in the hotel lobby for the Uber driver to bring my suitcase back. By the time I finally made it to my room, it was well past 1 a.m.

But here's where things get even worse: I woke up in the morning with a fever. A bad fever. I had no idea at the time it was Influenza A, but I knew something wasn't right.

Despite feeling like death warmed over, I wasn't about to let anything stop me from going to those breakout sessions. The very thing I was there for—to learn and grow.

Even though my fever was pushing 103 degrees, I kept my focus (as best I could). That week, I learned about something that would shape my journey—something called the Reticular Activating System (RAS).

Let's Get Nerdy for a Minute

The way you think about yourself, your business, and your goals has a huge impact on whether you succeed or struggle. Your thoughts shape your reality, so it's important to recognize just how powerful they really are.

This concept is based on how your brain works, specifically a part called the Reticular Activating System (RAS). The RAS is like the brain's filter—it helps you focus on what matters. When you focus on something, your RAS kicks in, highlighting opportunities related to that focus.

For example, when I was sick with the flu, my focus was still on learning and my vision for the future. Even though I felt awful, my brain was looking for ways to move me forward. I learned how important it was to shift my focus, not just in good times, but especially when the going got tough.

When you focus on your goals, your RAS helps you find more opportunities that align with those goals. If you focus on the negative—how hard things are, how many obstacles you face— guess what? Your brain will help you find more of that too.

Have you ever bought a new car and suddenly noticed that same model everywhere? That's your RAS at work. It's not that there are suddenly more of those cars on the road—your brain is simply noticing what you're focused on.

Mindset Matters

I could have easily fixated on the setbacks—on how much it hurt to lose my role and how sick I was on that trip. But instead, I kept my focus on learning and growing, because that was part of my vision.

Even though my physical body was exhausted and struggling, my mind was still working to connect the dots, build that vision, and push forward.

The moral of the story is that your mindset matters. Positive thinking isn't just about feeling good, it can actually change the way you show up in the world.

But the opposite is true too. If you're constantly telling yourself that you're not good enough or that success is out of reach, your brain will help you find reasons to reinforce that belief, and it can create a cycle that holds you back.

> **"… Fix your thoughts on what is true, and honorable, and right, and pure, and lovely, and admirable. Think about things that are excellent and worthy of praise."**
> Philippians 4:8 (NLT)

What are you focusing on today? Is it moving you closer to your vision or further away?

Hold On to Your Vision Through the Chaos

In my early years of building my business, I had four young daughters, a household to manage, and almost no time to myself. My life was filled with chaos—homeschooling, sports, dance classes, church activities, and more. Every day felt like a whirlwind. But there was one thing I always came back to: my vision.

When everything felt overwhelming, my vision kept me focused. It wasn't just a dream; it was my purpose, guiding me through those tough moments. When I focused on what mattered most, my RAS helped me find more ways to make it happen.

So, as I continued to face those challenges, whether it was lack of time or battling sickness, I kept my focus on what I could control, what I could learn, and what I could build.

You see, once I shifted my focus, my reality began to shift too. Those small moments of focused action—those small windows of time I carved out for my business—added up and helped me achieve success that I had only dreamed of.

When you're juggling a million responsibilities like I was, it's not about finding huge chunks of time. It's about making the most of the small moments and keeping your vision at the forefront of your mind, even in the chaos.

A Clear Vision Is Contagious

When people see your commitment to your vision, it can inspire them to join you and support your goals. That's when the opportunities really start coming. It could mean new customers, team members, or partnerships that help you grow your business.

When you're truly passionate about your vision and focused on making it happen, others naturally want to be part of that journey. They're drawn to your determination and the clarity of your purpose.

And don't forget to write it down, make a vision board, and review it regularly. When you focus on that vision every day, your RAS will help you continue to find the opportunities that align with it.

Choose Your Focus to Shape Your Future

Even when life throws you punches, even when it feels like everything is falling apart, the more you focus on your vision, the more it will become your reality.

Your thoughts shape your beliefs, your beliefs shape your actions, and those actions shape your future. When you intentionally choose to focus on the positive, on your vision, your RAS will help you find more of it.

Take a second to choose your thoughts carefully. Focus on the things that line up with your goals. When you do that, you'll start noticing how your reality begins to shift, one thought at a time. It's all about guiding your mind in the right direction—and with that, creating the future you desire.

I challenge you today: Write down your vision. Make it as vivid and detailed as possible. Place it somewhere you'll see it every day. Read it out loud each morning. Share it with someone who will support and encourage you.

Remember, your focus creates your future.

Key Takeaways to WIN

- **Your vision is your roadmap.** A clear vision keeps you focused, even when life gets tough. Stay connected to your "why" and let it guide you.

- **What you focus on grows.** Your thoughts shape your reality. Focus on your goals, not the obstacles, and you'll start noticing more opportunities.

- **Mindset matters.** Positive thinking isn't just motivational, it's powerful. When you focus on the good, your brain will help you find it.

- **Keep your vision alive.** Write it down, review it often, and let your vision inspire others. When you stay focused, your future becomes clearer.

I Dare You to Take Action

I dare you to get crystal clear on your vision.

You've learned all about the power of focus—how your vision shapes your future and why what you pay attention to matters. Now, it's time to take action.

Take a few minutes to answer these questions:

- What do I truly want for my future?
- Why does it matter to me?
- What small action can I take today to move closer to it?

Once you've answered those, I challenge you to write down your vision. Put it somewhere you'll see it every day—on your mirror, your phone screen, or your workspace. Then, take one step toward it this week. It doesn't have to be huge, just *intentional*.

When you commit to your vision, the opportunities, the people, and the path forward will start revealing themselves in ways you never imagined. Remember, what you focus on gets bigger.

Here's your challenge: Write it down. See it. Believe it. Then take action. Let's see what happens when you focus on creating the future you truly desire.

THE 3 Ds OF ENTREPRENEURSHIP

As a busy woman, it's easy to feel like you're drowning in tasks all the time. Throw in a business, and there's always something screaming for your attention. No matter how hard you try, there's just never enough time in the day to get everything done.

Believe me, I remember feeling like I was constantly burning the candle at both ends, trying to do it all: mom of four, wife, homeschool teacher, coach, church leader, and, of course, entrepreneur (let's not forget to add housekeeper, personal chef, and chauffeur into the mix!). Sound familiar?

I found myself in a never-ending cycle of insanity, *doing* so much yet still feeling like I wasn't making progress, mostly because I didn't really know where to start or how to prioritize.

Burned out and overwhelmed, I knew I had to shift my approach. I had to stop trying to handle everything by myself because there were only so many hours in the day.

Enter one of the best pieces of advice I ever received in my network marketing journey: **Do It, Dump It, or Delegate It.** This mind-shifting system came many years ago from a top leader in my former direct sales company. She trained us on a simple way to reshape how we run a direct sales business.

Her **3 Ds** strategy helped me develop a clear plan of action and get things done without sacrificing my health or sanity.

Now, you might be thinking, "Well, that sounds simple enough," but if you're an entrepreneur with ADHD tendencies like me, then your mind often races a million miles a minute.

Staying focused can be a real struggle, especially when juggling all the hats of a mom and an entrepreneur. I was constantly fighting the feeling of needing to do it all, and realizing I couldn't get it all done.

The 3 D system gave me the structure I desperately needed while still allowing me the flexibility to thrive. And the best part? It gave me the freedom to enjoy my business again. And now, I'm passing it on to you.

1. Do It

Have you ever woken up and felt like today's the day you're going to crush it? You've got that fire in your belly. You're motivated, fired up, and ready to tackle that to-do list—and, let's be honest, make some money while you're at it. But when you sit down, you're not even sure where to start?

The "Do It" part is all about focusing on the actions that will actually move your business forward. In network marketing, that means booking appointments, selling products, and recruiting new team members. These are the activities that drive success.

Until I grasped this, I was constantly spinning my wheels, trying to juggle it all. I didn't realize that the secret wasn't just in *doing more things* but in *doing the right things*.

Once I focused on three key activities that actually built my business—**booking, selling, and recruiting**—things started falling into place.

Focus on What You're Good At, but Do It All

Your business can sometimes feel overwhelming with so many moving parts. You might be amazing at recruiting but struggle with sales, or perhaps you're a booking pro but don't love the technical side of things.

Here's the deal: You don't have to be an expert at everything, but you do have to make sure you're covering all the bases for a well-rounded business.

For example, if you're not the greatest at recruiting, don't be afraid to use a recruiting video from someone in your company that you love who's had success! That's what I did early on. You can even use a recruiting funnel to simplify the process. A recruiting funnel weeds out the tire kickers and helps you connect with people who are considering your business opportunity. You could have them watch a short video and fill out a survey and capture their email so you can continue the conversation.

Want to see an example? Check out:

info.themakeupmimi.com

To watch a video showing you how to build your own recruiting funnel, visit:

recruitingfunnel.susannormanonline.com

If sales isn't your strong suit yet, use scripts or closing sheets to build confidence and improve your skills. It's okay to rely on resources and tools to bridge the gap—there's no shame in that game. It keeps things real and shows your prospects that what you do isn't so hard, especially if they see that you're simply reading a script. The goal, as shared earlier, is progress, not perfection.

Find Your Superpowers

The first step is to know what you're great at. What lights you up and makes you feel like a total rock star? What do you find yourself naturally drawn to and excited about?

For me, I've always LOVED coaching and working with people one-on-one. Recruiting, building relationships, and connecting with my team and customers energized me. So, I focused on that.

But remember, while your strengths should be your primary focus, you still need to make sure you're touching on all three core areas—booking, selling, and recruiting—every day. You can't skip any of them if you want sustained growth in your business.

So, what about you? What's your sweet spot?

- Are you the **social media maven**?
- A **queen of networking**?
- The **sales powerhouse**?
- A **recruiting rock star**?

Whatever you *love* and excel at, **double down on it**. That's where your time and energy should be focused. But don't forget, you'll still need to round out the rest of your business— *don't shy away from learning new skills or utilizing tools* that can help you with areas that aren't your strong suit.

By knowing and focusing on your strengths, it's not just more fun, but it also pushes your business forward faster. Everything else? Just distractions.

Get Out of the "Busy Work" Trap

Once you've figured out your strengths, it's time to *prioritize*. I remember the days when my to-do list was a mile long, and I felt like I was just checking boxes instead of actually making progress. The key is to ask yourself:

- Which ones will have the biggest impact?
- Will this task move my business forward?
- Will it bring me closer to my goals?

So, I started getting ruthless with my list. If a task didn't directly contribute to my big goals—booking, selling, or recruiting—I let it go. Trust me, when you focus on the core things, you won't get lost in the "busy work" and you'll reach your goals much faster!

Stay Focused

You want a real truth bomb? Distractions are everywhere. Hello? I know I'm not the only one who gets sucked into endless scrolling through social media reels, checking every notification, or spiraling into a rabbit hole of *"what if"* thoughts about the next shiny new idea! They're all competing for your attention. But if you really want to crush your goals, you've got to **stay focused**.

Here's a secret: **turn off the distractions**. Seriously … silence your phone, close unnecessary tabs on your browser, and maybe even put the social media apps away for a while.

There's even research now that shows performance significantly improves simply by putting your phone in another room. Even having it within reach—turned upside down or in your pocket or purse—impacts productivity. Isn't that wild?!

So, take control of your environment and create the space you need to truly focus. Your productivity will thank you for it!

To make things fun, I would turn it into a game and set a timer for 20–30 minutes to really get stuff done with intention. When you focus, you'll be amazed at how much more you get done. It's a little thing, but it makes a HUGE difference.

> **"Diligent hands will rule, but laziness ends in forced labor."**
> Proverbs 12:24 (NIV)

2. Dump It

We all have those things in our business that are no longer serving us. Events, tasks, and systems that once worked but now just drain our energy. I know I did! So, I began evaluating and getting rid of what wasn't helping my business grow.

Imagine you're at a buffet, tempted by all the delicious foods you see. But there's only so much you can fit on your plate. What do you do? You prioritize! You pick the food that you love, the ones that satisfy you, and leave the rest behind.

This also applies to your business. I can promise you, there are things you're trying to put on your plate that just don't fit. And it's holding you back! It's time, my friend, to take a hard look at those things.

Are you trying to do too much? Are you still holding on to old systems or ways of doing things that aren't working anymore? Let's take a minute and talk about those things you need to let go of and how to **dump them** for good.

Just Say No

One of the best lessons I learned on my network marketing journey was the power of saying "no." (Oh man, this was a tough one for me.) It took me *years* to get comfortable with it, and, to be honest, I still slip up sometimes!

I'm the type of person who has a hard time letting people down. *FOMO* is real, you know? That nagging voice in your head whispering, "But what if you miss the opportunity of a lifetime if you say no?!"

That's exactly what I would tell myself whenever someone asked me to take on something new. And because I *never* wanted to let anyone down, I'd say yes to everything, even if I didn't have the time or energy for it.

Here's the thing, though: It led straight to burnout. Fast. I was running on empty all the time, feeling like I was doing more and more … but I wasn't getting anywhere.

Turns out, saying yes to everything meant I was spreading myself so thin that I wasn't doing anything well. That's when I realized: to make room for the right opportunities, I had to *say no* to the wrong ones.

The truth is, the world won't end if you say no to a few things (even if that little voice in your head protests).

And, oh, how freeing that was!

Quit Wasting Time on Nonessential Tasks

I think it's safe to say that we've all been there—spending hours doing stuff that *feels* productive, but at the end of the day, you've gotten nothing done that really moves the needle in your business.

I used to spend so much time *rearranging* things or tweaking stuff that didn't need fixing. I call it creative avoidance. LOL! You know what I mean. Anything you can do to avoid the things you should be doing that maybe you're afraid of.

Let's not even talk about the never-ending cycle of checking email! It's easy to fall into this trap, but it's not helping you grow.

So, ask yourself, "What's sucking up my time but not contributing to my growth?" Are you …

- **Overthinking website tweaks or social media bios** that are perfectly fine, but you're stuck in the "I can make it better" loop?

- **Obsessing over the perfect script** rather than using it and tweaking it along the way based on feedback and experience?

- **Spending hours on low-value tasks** like creating flyers or perfecting business cards, instead of focusing on money-making activities like outreach and sales?

If so, I challenge you to become more aware of where your time is going and start taking *purposeful* action toward what truly moves the needle in your business.

Let It Go!

It's easy to get attached to systems because they're familiar. I mean, I can't be the only one who does this. But let's face it, that old printer you've had since 2004? It's not pulling its weight anymore.

And here's the reality: if it's not serving your business, it's time to say "goodbye." (If you're anything like me, you're now bobbing your head and singing along.)

For me, I had to let go of old systems that weren't working anymore. My team and I started using tools that streamlined our processes, making things quicker and more efficient, as I shared in the "Automate to Accelerate" chapter earlier in the book.

Think about this: *What systems or tools are you holding onto because they're "familiar" but just aren't cutting it anymore?*

Time to **dump** outdated systems. You need tools that will empower you, not slow you down. Sometimes that means upgrading your systems and getting rid of the old stuff that's holding you back. It might cost a little time or money now, but in the long run, it's worth it.

Ditch the Distractions

Don't feel like you have to be a superhero and take on every responsibility that comes your way. Ask yourself, "What activities am I doing that seem important but are actually taking me away from my business focus and ultimately the vision for my future?"

If something doesn't line up with your goals, it's time to *dump it*.

Don't let distractions keep you from what really matters. Remember, you don't have to be everywhere, do everything, or hold on to things that no longer serve you.

Lastly, saying "no" when it counts will leave you with way more energy for the things that are most important and empower you to build the business you've always wanted!

So go on, be bold! I dare you! *Dump it*—and watch what happens!

3. Delegate It

Alright, here's the sanity saver: **Delegate It**! I have to admit, this one was tough for me too. I had the mentality that if I didn't do it myself, it wouldn't get done right. But I learned quickly that trying to do everything myself was impossible to maintain.

I had to constantly remind myself, "*Susan, you can't (and shouldn't) do everything yourself.*" As much as we might like to think we're superwoman, we're not! There are tasks that absolutely need to be done to maintain harmony in our life and business, but *some-one else* can do them, and probably better. So, I started *trusting* others with the tasks that weren't the best use of my time or skills.

When you delegate, you create space to scale your business, enjoy your work, and avoid burnout. Who doesn't want more of that? But how do you delegate effectively? Well, I've got you covered. Here are a few tips to help you pass off tasks without the guilt trip:

Don't Waste Dollar Time on Penny Tasks

You absolutely cannot afford to waste **dollar time on penny activities.** There are things in your day that may seem necessary but aren't where you should be spending your precious time and energy. These tasks eat up your time but don't directly help your business grow.

Here are some tasks you can delegate:

- **Household chores.** Yep, hire someone to clean your house or mow the lawn!

- **Social media management.** Use automated party posting services or a virtual assistant (VA) to help with that—someone who knows how to create, schedule, and engage.

- **Office help.** If you have teenagers, they can help pack orders, track inventory, or enter sales tickets.

- **Email management.** I hired a VA service specific to my company, which handled tasks such as managing weekly emails, team recognition on Facebook, and birthday or anniversary wishes.

- **Childcare.** Juggling toddlers while working? Hire a sitter or nanny a couple of days a week, even if it's just a few hours, to focus on business.

See what I mean? There are a ton of things you can delegate. I've just named a few. You can even get your kids involved in some of this to help take the load off. That's what I did. It was a family business, after all, and everyone helped out.

Believe me, you'll be much better off spending your time on tasks that generate income and grow your team. You may not be able to do them all, but start somewhere with a few that would help you free up some time.

Find the Right People

You can't just pass off any task to anyone. You've got to find the right people. This is huge.

Look for someone who:

- **has the skills** for the job (obvious, right?)
- **is reliable** (they can actually meet deadlines)
- **understands your business**

If you hire someone to help you with your social media and email, make sure they can write in your voice. This is crucial to building a brand.

Whether you're bringing on a virtual assistant, freelancer, family volunteer, or a team member, make sure they're the right fit for the job. Otherwise, you'll spend more time *fixing* mistakes than you would doing it yourself. No thank you.

Communicate, Communicate, Communicate

Once you've found your person, you need to communicate clearly. No mind-reading here! Be specific about what needs to be done and set deadlines. No one likes being left in the dark. Make sure they know:

- what's expected
- the exact timeline for delivery
- any boundaries you have

For example, when I got some social media help from my daughter, I was very specific about the kind of content I wanted, the tone, the times I wanted posts to go live, and what kind of posts were off-limits. Being clear up front saves you time, frustration, and confusion later.

Provide Feedback

I know it can be hard to let go of control, but micromanaging your people only leads to more stress and burnout. They may not do it exactly the same way you would, but trust the process—they'll probably surprise you. The more you let them shine, the more you'll both grow.

Don't forget to check in, ask questions, or offer feedback when needed. Start with something positive like, "You did an amazing job with the Instagram stories last week. I loved how you featured customer testimonials—it really brought a personal touch!" A little praise goes a long way.

Then, if something does need to change or improve, be constructive but also be kind. This honesty builds mutual respect and helps keep things on track to maintain a smoothly running business.

Building on the example above, you might continue by saying, "The only thing I'd tweak is maybe adding more behind-the-scenes content so followers feel more connected to the day-to-day of my business. What do you think?"

As you continue to give feedback and guide your team, you'll start to see how important it is to step back and let others take ownership. It's a balance of providing direction and then giving them the freedom to run with it. This is where delegating starts to pay off.

Work Smarter, Not Harder

As I delegated more, I realized how much I really needed a team, and honestly, they did it way better than I could have! Letting my team do what they love made them feel valued and gave me what I needed too. It was a true WIN-WIN!

Your time is precious. Don't waste it trying to do everything yourself. Delegate, and watch your business grow!

The 3 Ds—**Do It, Dump It, and Delegate It**—are a simple yet powerful strategy designed to help you work smarter, not harder. By focusing on the things that matter most, clearing out distractions, and trusting others with the rest, you're setting yourself up to *win big*!

Remember, it's not about doing everything; it's about doing the *important things* with purpose and intention. So, ditch the stress, implement the 3 Ds, and start building the business you've always dreamed of. Your future self will thank you!

Key Takeaways to WIN

- **Do it.** Focus on what you're great at and what truly lights you up.

- **Dump it.** Let go of tasks, systems, and activities that don't move the needle or line up with your goals.

- **Delegate it.** Pass on the necessary tasks that don't require your personal touch, giving others the chance to shine.

I Dare You to Take Action

I dare you to *Do it. Dump it. Delegate it.*

You've learned the 3 Ds. Now it's time to move from knowing to doing.

Ask yourself:

- What are the top income-producing tasks I need to do daily?
- What distractions or tasks do I need to dump?
- What can I delegate to free up time and energy?

Here's your challenge:

Set a timer for 10 minutes. Write everything on your plate and label each task: Do It, Dump It, or Delegate It. Then, this week, commit to following through.

When you focus on the right work and release what doesn't serve you, you stop running in circles. Take control of your time, work with intention, and watch momentum build. No need to work harder than necessary.

MASTERING THE FIVE AREAS OF SELF- LEADERSHIP

*I*magine stepping into your power, confidently leading your own life and business. You're unstoppable—not just because of your skills, but with the strength that comes from within. That's self-leadership.

There's a saying that goes:

You cannot teach what you do not know, and you cannot lead where you will not go.

In other words, how can you lead others if you aren't leading yourself well?

Self-leadership is about taking accountability for your own life—making choices and taking actions that align with your goals and values. It's about leading with purpose and intent.

As a business woman, focusing on five key areas of self-leadership—money, time, health, habits, and relationships—forms the foundation for success and happiness. When you master these, you can show up with confidence in your business and life.

So, what do you say? Ready to grow? Great, let's jump in.

1. Money

Money is more than something you work for—it's a tool. It can either fuel your growth or keep you stuck. Learning to manage it well isn't just a business skill; it's a life skill.

I know what it's like to feel buried in debt. My credit was so bad, I couldn't even get a credit card to run my business.

Asking for help felt humiliating, but I reached out to a mentor. We spent hours going through my finances, and I started making small but intentional changes—creating a budget, tracking my spending, and using tools like the EveryDollar app (I *highly recommend it, by the way*).

Step by step, I took control and climbed out of that financial hole.

People love to say, "*Money is the root of all evil*," but that's just not true. It's the *love* of money that creates problems. But honestly? Money is a tool, and how you use it determines its impact.

And let's be real—money matters. I've lived without money, and I've lived with it, and life with it? Way easier. Why? Because it gives you more choices, peace of mind, and the ability to make a greater impact. It's not about greed, it's about freedom and possibility.

Money mindset: Start by changing how you see money. Move from scarcity to abundance. Instead of feeling guilty about wanting more, remind yourself: *I am worthy of abundance.*

Practical Tips:

- Open a separate bank account for your business. It makes tracking income and expenses way easier.

- Don't forget taxes! (*Ugh, I know.*) Learn about them, or hire a pro. It's an investment that pays off in the long run.

Giving changes everything. It sounds backward, right? When money is tight, giving it away can feel impossible. But generosity isn't just about helping others. It transforms YOU.

When I started giving 10% of my income to my church, I was scared. But the blessings that followed? Unreal. Suddenly, I wasn't just surviving, I was thriving. Doors opened, opportunities appeared, and things started falling into place. Giving taught me trust, rewired my mindset, and made me a magnet for abundance.

Giving didn't just change my finances—it changed me.

Once you've taken control of your finances, the next area that often steals our success is our time.

2. Time

Time is one of the most valuable resources we have. Once it's gone, you can't get it back, so managing it effectively is key to success.

- **Time audit:** Take a hard look at how you spend your time. Are you being intentional with it? Or are you scrolling through social media or binge-watching Netflix? The more intentional you are with your time, the more you'll get done, and the better you'll feel about it.

- **Power hour:** Set aside one hour to focus solely on income-producing activities (IPAs)—sales calls, appointments, or recruiting. Try it and see how much you can get done in 60 minutes.

If the Power Hour isn't your style, try time-blocking. Set aside specific blocks of time for tasks—30 minutes for emails, an hour for meetings, etc. Use a weekly plan sheet to organize your schedule and minimize distractions.

- **Setting boundaries:** Protect your time by setting boundaries. Learn to say no, whether it's to clients or friends who want to steal your focus. For example, I decided years ago that Sundays were off-limits for work. That decision has helped me recharge and spend time with family.

Mastering time isn't just about crossing things off a list, it's about balance. Celebrate your wins, make room for rest, and enjoy the process.

3. Health

Without your health, what do you really have? One of the biggest lessons I've learned is the importance of prioritizing health before it becomes a crisis.

There's a saying that says, "If you don't make time for your health, you'll be forced to make time for your sickness," a lesson I learned back in 2018.

After battling anemia for years, I had a health scare that changed everything. I nearly didn't make it to the hospital after a serious life-threatening medical event occurred while I was working a home party. That experience made me realize how dangerous it is to neglect your health.

- **Prioritize self-care:** Your health is the foundation of everything you do. Make it a priority now, before it's too late. Regular exercise, healthy eating, and enough sleep are essential for maintaining energy and focus.

- **Systems in place:** When I had to take six weeks off to recover, I realized the importance of building systems to keep things running smoothly even when life throws curveballs.

- **Community:** Surround yourself with people who care about health and wellness too. Whether it's joining a fitness class or going on a wellness retreat, being around like-minded people keeps you motivated.

Your business can wait. Your health can't.

Now that we've covered money, time, and health, let's talk about what drives your daily actions—your habits.

4. Habits

Habits are the building blocks of success. They turn intentions into actions and actions into results. It takes consistency to form new habits—don't expect them to happen overnight.

- **Assess your habits:** Are any of your current habits holding you back? Maybe you're hitting snooze too much, avoiding follow-ups, or getting distracted by social media. Take a look at your habits and identify the ones that aren't serving you.

- **Replace negative habits:** Once you identify the habits you need to change, replace them with new ones that align with your goals. For example, if you procrastinate on follow-ups, schedule them into your day.

- **Set your environment for success:** Your environment plays a huge role in habit formation. Want to prospect every day? Set aside 30 minutes in the morning and have your tools ready to go. A designated space for specific tasks helps you stay focused and efficient.

Be patient with yourself as you work on building better habits. Change takes time. Celebrate your small wins, and keep pushing forward.

5. Relationships

Building strong relationships is key to both personal and business success. Your network is everything—the people you invest in will help you grow.

- **Listen actively:** Good communication is the foundation of strong relationships. Practice active listening—don't just wait for your turn to talk. Ask questions and try to understand the other person's perspective. People value being heard, and it builds trust.

- **Feedback and growth:** Communication is a two-way street. Be open to feedback and growth. Don't let defensiveness get in the way of improvement. Be willing to have those tough conversations, because often, they lead to stronger connections.

- **Give as much as you get:** Relationships aren't just about what you can take; they're about what you can give. Offer help, support, and kindness without expecting anything in return. It'll come back to you in ways you least expect. As Maya Angelou said, "People won't remember what you said, but they will remember how you made them feel."

- **Inner circle:** Spend time with people who truly support and understand you. These are the relationships that will keep you grounded and motivated through the highs and lows of business and life.

Mastering these five areas of self-leadership—money, time, health, habits, and relationships—is a lifelong journey. But by focusing on these areas, you can build a life and business that truly reflect your goals and values. Self-leadership isn't about being perfect—it's about progress. Keep improving, and success will follow.

Key Takeaways to WIN

- **Money.** Take control of your finances by shifting your mindset, creating a budget, and setting financial goals. It's not just about how much you earn, but how you manage it.

- **Time.** Time is precious—manage it wisely by setting priorities, creating systems, and setting boundaries to create a healthy work-life balance.

- **Health.** Prioritize your health with exercise, healthy food, and enough sleep. When you feel your best, you show up better in every area of your life.

- **Habits.** Build habits that support your goals. Replace negative ones, create a positive environment, and remember that change takes time.

- **Relationships.** Strong relationships come from good communication. Listen actively, speak clearly, and surround yourself with people who support your growth.

I Dare You to Take Action

I dare you to master self-leadership.

You've explored the five key areas of self-leadership: money, time, health, habits, and relationships. These are foundational to how you show up in life and business.

Stop waiting for the perfect moment. Starting today, lead yourself with intention.

Ask yourself:

- Which area needs my attention most right now?
- What small, intentional change can I make today?
- What habit or system would support my long-term success?

Here's your challenge:

Choose ONE area of self-leadership and take a bold step forward this week. Don't overthink it. Just begin. Progress happens in the doing.

When you lead yourself well, everything else follows. Step up, take control, and lead yourself to the next level.

**"Whoever can be trusted with very little
can also be trusted with much ..."**
(Luke 10:16, NIV)

PERSISTENCE IS KEY

When I say we came from humble beginnings, I mean it. I remember when my kids were little, we couldn't even afford to heat our home. We'd rely on our oven and a tiny kerosene heater just to stay warm.

There were times when I'd keep the girls in the car after errands, just to let the house warm up before going inside. It was tough, but we learned valuable lessons from it—lessons in perseverance and grit. We learned that nothing worth having comes easy.

Getting married at 18 and having two kids by 19, we quickly realized that nothing would be handed to us. We had to work hard for everything. Over time, I came to understand that the people who truly succeed are often those who have come from nothing or faced major hardships. They didn't give up—and neither did we.

I see now that those incredibly hard moments shaped us and helped me grow as a leader. **I believe God uses those struggles to refine our character and test our perseverance.**

It's almost as if God (through my circumstances) was asking me, "Are you truly committed to your dreams? Do you have the grit to keep going when it gets tough?" I also believe that without those challenges, we would have never understood the responsibility of leadership.

The Bible says:

" … to whom much was given, of him much will be required … " Luke 12:48 (ESV)

The journey of an entrepreneur is filled with ups and downs—more downs than we'd care to admit. But without adversity, how could we ever truly empathize with someone else's struggles?

I remember going out with some business friends one night, hoping that some of their success would rub off on us. We scraped together what little we had and ended up at Denny's, ordering the cheapest thing on the menu, praying our card wouldn't get declined. When it did, I was so embarrassed, but I knew I couldn't give up. I had to keep going.

Shortly after that, our electricity got shut off. Sitting in the dark with my kids, I kept myself together, and I vowed they wouldn't know how tough things were. I didn't want to ask our parents for help; I felt like this was a battle we had to fight ourselves. It was hard, but **some battles help you grow.** It's those very struggles that shape us into who we become.

As time went on, my direct sales business became a lifeline—not just for the money—but for securing a better future for our family. We went through many setbacks, but I kept moving forward, knowing that even slow progress was still progress.

Today, when I reflect on everything we've been through—from near foreclosure to facing financial ruin—I feel a sense of gratitude. Those tough moments built resilience and taught me that, as the saying goes, **"Success is not final, failure is not fatal; it's the courage to continue that counts."**

No one has it all figured out from the start. Life's a journey with hills and valleys. When you're in the valley, it's easy to feel defeated. And when times get tough, I remember *it's my choice to keep going,* and I believe you'll choose to keep going too. Persistence is the key.

The Key to Becoming an Expert

To truly master something, it takes time. *Lots* of time. To become an expert at something, you need 10,000 hours. That's right, *10,000* hours. Let that sink in for a moment.

Now, I'm not saying you need to count every single hour and track them like a mad scientist, but let me tell you, when I think about those 10,000 hours of practice, it reminds me of a time in my life when I *really* had to grind.

It was eighth grade, and I was sitting in band class when Mr. Ebert dropped the bomb: "All-county band auditions are next month!" Oh boy. There I was, brand new to the clarinet, feeling like I was totally out of my league.

Most of my friends had been playing since fourth grade, and I was the rookie trying to avoid embarrassing myself in front of everyone. I knew I wasn't qualified, but hey, what was I going to do? Back out? Not a chance.

So I did what any self-respecting eighth-grader would do: I practiced. And practiced. And practiced some more. Every single day. I poured my heart into those notes, blowing my lungs out and making sure my fingers hit every note just right. There were days when I felt like giving up. There were days I questioned if I even had the talent to make it. But I kept showing up.

The day of the audition came. I walked into that room with my clarinet, all set to perform for the judge. *Here we go,* I thought. I played my heart out, giving it everything I had. One note after another. It felt like I was playing perfectly—or at least, I *thought* I was.

A few weeks later, I got called into the band director's office. He looked at me, all serious, and said, "So, Susan, how much did you pay the judge?"

With a feeling of confusion, I asked, "*Why?*"

"Because you got the highest score in the entire county!" he said.

I couldn't believe it! *First chair.* First clarinet in the All-County band.

Truthfully? It wasn't about being naturally gifted. It wasn't about some magical spark of talent that I was born with. It was about hours of practice, of showing up when I didn't feel like it, pushing myself past the doubt. I was determined to keep going, no matter how tough it got.

Mastery takes time in business too. There's no "overnight success." You have to put in the hours, face rejection, and learn from every experience. You have to keep playing the notes, even when you're unsure if you're doing it right.

Just like I had to play the clarinet for hours until my fingers could do it without thinking, you'll have to keep showing up to develop your skills in marketing, sales, and leadership.

Trust me, there's nothing more rewarding than looking back and realizing that all those small steps—those tiny moments of practice—added up to something big. It's the same feeling I had when I walked into that room and found out I was first chair.

Get Specific with Your Goals

Fast-forward to the beginning of one of my direct sales journeys. I know this sounds ridiculous, but I set a goal to visit 1,000 houses. But hear me out—I knew that much *was* attainable.

I also knew that I couldn't control how many customers I'd get, how much I'd sell, or how many people would join my team. But I *could* control how many people I introduced myself to.

I'm a numbers person, so here's my logic: Even if I only got a 1% return on my effort, it would still be worth it. Ten customers? That could turn into something huge. One opportunity leads to another.

So, I ordered 1,000 samples and 1,000 little postcard flyers to hand out. My mentor called me to double-check that I didn't accidentally order 1,000 samples by mistake (I think she was worried I'd go bankrupt on a whim). But nope, I was serious. I needed to get out there and meet people however I could.

The plan wasn't to make big sales on the spot—it was about making connections. I mapped out my neighborhood and set my sights on hitting up the area within a ten-mile radius. July heat? No problem. I had bills to pay and a dream to chase, and I wasn't backing down.

Going from house to house, I knocked on doors, introduced myself, handed out samples with my flyer, and told them, "If you ever need anything, I'm right here!" It wasn't glamorous, but it worked.

I even hit up a local wellness center, asked if I could drop off a lead box, and offered to promote their business in exchange. That connection, plus the 1,000 houses, started to pay off.

One of the women I met even became a customer and eventually helped me build my team. By the end of August, I had eight active team members—enough to start the leadership qualification process. And we finished that qualification in just two months, which was something that took laser focus and commitment to complete.

Focus on the Activity, Not the Result

Here's what I learned: You can't control who says yes, but you *can* control how many people you show up for.

Success is in the *doing*. When you focus on the process instead of the results, you win. Consistency and effort will always lead to progress.

As an introvert, I never imagined myself doing anything like this, but the need was real, and I wasn't about to give up. It started with a dream and the will to win. With those two things, anything's possible.

If you're struggling to see results, don't give up. Keep going. Keep learning. Keep showing up. The more you practice, the closer you get to becoming the expert you want to be. Those 10,000 hours? They don't have to be perfect. But they do need to be consistent.

What Helped Me Persist

1. A Strong Foundation in Faith

Faith was the lifeline. When my circumstances screamed at me to *give up*, I leaned on Philippians 4:13 (NIV): "I can do all things through Christ who strengthens me."

When facing seemingly insurmountable challenges, faith reminded me that I'm never alone. It shifted my perspective from what's happening *to* me to what's happening *for* me.

And when you're holding on to a divine promise, you begin to see each setback not as a failure, but as an opportunity for growth, learning, and resilience.

Believing in a purpose greater than me also gave me the strength to keep pushing even when I was exhausted, frustrated, and questioning whether I was on the right path.

2. A Calling to Overcome

I didn't just believe I was meant to overcome for my own benefit—I believed my struggles could inspire others. Every challenge I faced, every obstacle I had to conquer, gave me a clearer sense of purpose. I realized that by pushing through my struggles, I could show others that they, too, could rise above their circumstances.

There's power in knowing that your journey isn't just about *you*. It's about lifting others as you climb. When you're faced with challenges, remind yourself that overcoming them isn't just about your success—it's about the impact you'll have on others who are looking to you for hope and inspiration. You might be one breakthrough away from changing someone's life. And that is worth fighting for.

Questions for You

What's holding you back? Do you believe that you're not capable? That's a lie! You are fully equipped for success. Every challenge you've faced has prepared you for what's next.

Are you playing the victim, making excuses, or blaming others? It's easy to say, "If only things were different, I'd be successful," but success is about how you respond to challenges. Stop blaming and start owning your journey. Commitment means showing up, even when it's tough.

Dreams vs. Actions

It's easy to talk about your big dreams and how much you want them. But dreams alone won't get you anywhere.

"…faith without works is dead …" (James 2:26, KVJ)

A dream without action is just a wish. It's kind of like hoping a pizza would magically appear on your doorstep because you imagined it, without actually ordering one. (We've all been there, dreaming up a perfect scenario, but not doing anything about it.)

You can dream all day, but unless you take steps to make those dreams a reality, they'll stay just that—dreams.

It's like reading a recipe and having all the ingredients, but never actually cooking the meal. You're left with a pile of stuff that could turn into something amazing … but never does because you aren't willing to put in the work.

Success isn't accidental, it's the result of consistent effort. You can read all the books and collect all the knowledge, but if you don't act on it, you won't move forward. It's about putting in the work, pushing past the doubt, even when you don't feel like it.

I can teach you exactly what to do and how to do it, but the real question is: are you ready to put in the work? To take action, even when it's tough?

If you're not ready to take those steps, all the advice in the world won't matter. You'll just be collecting dust. If you want to make those dreams a reality, you have to do more than wish. You have to *work*.

The journey is messy and imperfect, but persistence is everything. Your struggles don't define you—they shape you into who you're meant to become. Keep moving forward, even when it's hard. Your breakthrough is waiting on the other side. So, are you ready to put in the work?

Key Takeaways to WIN

- **Persistence pays off.** Success isn't instant. Life's going to throw curveballs. Keep pushing forward, even when things get tough. Small steps, over time, lead to big results.

- **Mastery takes time (and practice).** Success is more about practice than talent. It takes 10,000 hours to become an expert. It's not about being naturally gifted, but about showing up and putting in the work consistently.

- **Struggles don't define you.** Tough times don't define who you are; they strengthen you. Keep going, and you'll grow through your challenges.

- **Faith keeps you going.** When things get hard, faith in a bigger purpose will fuel your persistence, help you keep moving forward, and remind you that quitting isn't an option.

I Dare You to Take Action

I dare you to keep going.

You've seen how perseverance turns hard seasons into powerful lessons. Now it's your turn. Keep going—even when the road gets rough.

Ask yourself:

- Where have I felt discouraged or close to quitting?
- What obstacle am I ready to push through?
- Am I willing to keep showing up, even when progress feels slow?

Here's your challenge:

Choose one area where you've been discouraged and take one action today. Send the follow-up. Make the call. Take the step that scares you.

Persistence requires continuing to show up. Success lives on the other side of difficulty, and the breakthrough you're looking for may be closer than you think.

DON'T LET FEAR WIN

I remember when I was a brand-new consultant in my former direct sales business, dreaming of becoming a Sales Director. I wanted it so badly—I could see myself leading, inspiring, and helping other women change their lives by building something incredible. But there was one tiny problem.

Sales Directors had to travel.

And I had a terrible fear of flying.

I told myself I couldn't do it. The thought of getting on a plane made my heart race and my stomach turn. Fear had a grip on me, whispering every possible worst-case scenario. For a while, I believed it. I let the fear sink in, whispering doubts that almost held me back from moving up the career path.

But my unit leader was smart. She didn't push the flying issue because she knew it terrified me. Instead, she focused on my dreams and goals, keeping me moving forward. She waited until I crossed the finish line before she stretched me even more, helping me see that fear didn't have to be the thing that stopped me.

And that's the thing about fear—it's a sneaky thing. It loves to disguise itself as a perfectly logical reason to stay put. Fear can creep up in so many ways.

- **Procrastination** (I'll start when I feel ready.)
- **Self-doubt** (What if I fail?)
- **Comfort zone excuses** (I'm fine where I am.)

But most of the time, the real reason we stay stuck comes down to fear—fear of failure, fear of rejection, fear of stepping outside the boundaries of what we know. It's far easier to stay in your comfort zone, playing it safe, than it is to face the raw truth of where you are and own up to where you're not.

Quite honestly, if you let fear control your decisions, you're giving away your power. You're letting fear decide whether you try, whether you step up, and whether you reach for something better.

Overcoming Fear of Judgment

Can we just be real for a second? The fear of judgment is admittedly a HUGE barrier to showing up authentically. And it's natural to worry about what others think of you. But here's something I've learned that has personally helped me a ton: other people's opinions of me are none of my business.

A wise person once said, "If their opinion doesn't match your purpose, then it doesn't matter." Boom. Mic drop.

It doesn't matter if someone thinks your business idea is crazy or if they don't understand why you're so passionate about it. Why let them mess with the dreams that God placed in your heart?

If their opinion doesn't align with your dreams, don't let it slow you down. Focus on your goals, your values, and your purpose, and let the judgment slide off your back.

When you're clear on what you want, ignoring the noise from others becomes a lot easier. Remember, your goals matter more than what anyone else thinks.

The Power of a Made-Up Mind

There's something unstoppable about a person who decides to change their life.

Not just someone who wishes for it. Not someone who hopes for it. I'm talking about a person who draws a line in the sand, looks their excuses square in the face, and says, "No more. I'm all in."

When someone gets to that place? Get out of the way because they're about to move mountains.

Let me tell you about my daughter, Amber. She was the quiet one. The soft-spoken girl who, for most of her childhood, wouldn't even go into the post office alone because she was too shy to talk to strangers.

But shy doesn't mean small.

When she was 12, Amber auditioned for a performing arts high school. She recorded a couple of songs with a professional backing track, and her vocals were so good the school called me after and asked for the raw version—just to make sure it was real.

At 15, she auditioned for *The Voice*. She didn't make it through, but she didn't quit either.

At 19, she joked with a friend in Knoxville, Tennessee, about starting a band. Most people would've laughed and moved on. But Amber? She packed up, drove to Knoxville, and recorded music.

That little "joke" became Pink Blush—an indie band with songs on every major streaming platform. Albums. Interviews. Monthly Shows. Fans.

But none of that happened by accident.

Amber decided.

She set the goal.

She did the work.

And it changed her life.

Your Business Isn't That Different

I know what you might be thinking: That's a cool story, but what does that have to do with me and my business?

Everything.

Because in this industry—direct sales, network marketing, entrepreneurship—we all start a little unsure. A little afraid. A little shy.

You sign up. You're excited. And then … life hits. The doubts sneak in. People make fun. You get your first "no." Maybe even a few.

Before you know it, you're dipping your toes in, instead of diving in. Waiting for "the right time." Waiting until you "feel ready." Waiting until you have more money, or more time, or more confidence.

But friend, success doesn't wait.

Success shows up for the ones who commit before they have it all figured out.

If you treat this business like a hobby, it will pay you like one.

If you treat it like an option, it will give you optional results.

But if you treat it like a decision—a line-in-the-sand, burn-the-boats, "this is happening no matter what" kind of decision—then you'll watch your entire life start to change.

It's not about talent.

It's not about luck.

It's about commitment.

Amber didn't become an artist because she was born confident. She became confident because she showed up scared and kept going anyway.

Set the Goal. Do the Work. Change Your Life.

Let's take this from story to strategy. Here's how you take the same kind of decisive energy and apply it to your business:

1. Decide What You Really Want

Not just "I want to be successful." That's too vague. Do you want to earn $10K/month? Retire your spouse? Send your kids to private school?

2. Set a Nonnegotiable Deadline

"I will hit this goal by [specific date]." Not maybe. Not hopefully. Write it down. Speak it out loud. Treat it like it's happening.

3. Break It Into Daily Steps

What do you need to do today, this week, and this month to move closer to that goal? DMs. Follow-ups. Booking events. Showing up on video. Make the plan—and follow it.

4. Eliminate the Option to Quit

Burn the boats. There is no "let's see if this works." The only option: Make it work.

5. Commit to Showing Up—No Matter What

Yes, it'll be hard sometimes. Yes, you'll have days where you question it all. But that's where the magic happens—when you show up anyway.

Fear Is an Illusion

Now, I'm not saying this is easy. Dreams feel scary, right? Sometimes, they seem impossible. You think about them, and your heart races. Your stomach knots up, and that little voice in your head whispers all the reasons it won't work.

But most of the time, fear is just an illusion. It's like a shadow that seems bigger than it really is. The moment you take action, you realize it's nothing more than a trick of the mind.

It's like walking into a dark room. You're scared, but when you turn the light on, you see there is nothing to be afraid of. FEAR is just **False Evidence Appearing Real**—the stories we tell ourselves that make our dreams seem scarier than they really are. But once you move through the fear and take that first step, you'll realize you had the strength all along.

I wish I could tell you that overcoming fear was a one-and-done deal, but truthfully, it never fully goes away. That's not a bad thing! Fear just means you are continuing to grow and stretch out of your comfort zone!

Faith or Fear?

Both faith and fear require belief in something you can't see. The question is, which one are you going to choose?

Scripture reminds us:

> **"Don't be afraid, for I am with you.**
> **Don't be discouraged, for I am your God.**
> **I will strengthen you and help you. I will hold**
> **you up with my victorious right hand."**
> Isaiah 41:10 (NLT)

When you choose faith over fear, you're choosing to lean on God's strength instead of your own. God's plan isn't for you to live stuck in fear—He's with you, strengthening you every step of the way. It may sound crazy, but confidence comes from action, and action is actually the antidote to fear.

When you start with small, courageous steps, you build momentum. Fear fades when you prove to yourself that you can do hard things.

Breaking the Fear Cycle

One of my biggest weapons against fear is learning. I've seen its transformative power not only in my own life but also in my team members and even my own daughters.

The more you know, the less power fear has over you. Knowledge fills the gaps where uncertainty—and therefore fear—likes to hide.

When I first started my business, I was terrified of rejection and looking foolish. But with each training I attended and each book I read, those fears began to shrink.

So, where should you start? I recommend:

- **Read books** by people who've walked the path before you.
- **Listen to podcasts** that expand your mindset and skills.
- **Get in the room** with people who have already done what you want to do.

The more you invest in yourself through learning, the stronger your confidence becomes. But knowledge alone isn't enough—the key to breaking the fear cycle is taking action.

This creates a powerful upward spiral: The more you act, the more confident you become. And that confidence becomes one of your best weapons against fear. Each small success builds evidence that you can do this.

In business, I've found there are three core fears that tend to keep people stuck:

1. **Lack of belief in your product** (Is it really worth sharing?)
2. **Lack of belief in your opportunity** (Can people actually succeed with this?)
3. **Lack of belief in yourself** (Am I capable of making this work?)

So, how do we tackle these limiting beliefs? Let's start by getting real about what's happening. We're held back because of things we don't fully understand, things that feel uncertain, or situations that push us outside our comfort zone.

These thoughts are simply signals that you're growing. When you look at it through that lens, you can move through it rather than letting it stop you. Learning gives you clarity, action gives you confidence, and together they give you the momentum to push past your fears and build the business you're capable of.

Here's how to shift from being held back by limiting beliefs to moving forward with confidence:

1. Know Your Why

When you know your "why," fear becomes easier to handle.

Your "why" is what gets you out of bed when you'd rather stay under the covers and keeps you pushing when things get tough.

Maybe your "why" is paying the bills without stress. Maybe it's saving for that family vacation, or proving to yourself that you can succeed.

When that's your reason, fear has less control. Because you're not just building a business, you're doing it for the people you love and the future you're fighting for.

2. Believe in Your Product and Opportunity

If fear comes from doubting what you're offering, ask yourself:

- Do I truly believe in this product?
- Do I see the value in what I'm sharing?

Because if you don't believe in it, no one else will either.

When it comes to your opportunity, you've got to be *all in*. Your belief should be so strong that no opinion, no rejection, no temporary setback can shake it.

3. Build Confidence in Yourself
A lot of times, fear isn't about the product or the opportunity—it's about *you*.

Maybe you're worried about what people will think. Maybe you're afraid of looking like you don't know what you're doing.

But here's the truth: **Other people's opinions don't pay your bills.**

If you're looking for advice, make sure it's from people who've been where you want to go. If you wouldn't trade places with them, don't take advice from them.

Confidence Is Magnetic
Your unique qualities—your personality, your story, your vibe—are the things that set you apart. I can't stress this enough: when you own what makes you *different*, your confidence becomes magnetic.

Focus on your passions. When you're passionate about something, you will naturally put your heart into it. Your passion is your superpower for attracting the right clients and teammates. If you love what you do, it'll show—and that's what makes you more relatable.

Your confidence will show others that you believe in your abilities and what you bring to the table. It doesn't mean arrogance or that you've got it all figured out (trust me, none of us do).

But when you show up with confidence, you give others the confidence to believe in you and your business. This not only helps you build strong relationships with clients and teammates but also gives you the courage to take on new challenges and grow.

Your Dreams Are Bigger Than Your Fears

Are there days when the fear of failure knocked me down? Of course! The fear of not being good enough, or of not being able to juggle everything. Would my business actually work? Was I putting my family at risk by chasing my dreams? Those thoughts popped up all the time.

But here's the thing I learned: **fear doesn't have to control you.** You can move forward even when fear is standing right next to you. You don't have to wait for it to disappear—you just have to decide to take the next step anyway.

Fear will never fully go away, but that doesn't mean it gets to win.

Feel the fear, acknowledge it, and then take action anyway. Because when you do, you'll look back one day and realize the thing you were so afraid of was never bigger than your dreams in the first place.

Key Takeaways to WIN

- **A made-up mind is your superpower.** Success starts the moment you stop *wishing* and start *deciding*. When you go all in, things begin to shift.

- **Confidence comes from doing, not waiting.** You don't wait to feel ready—you grow by doing it scared.

- **Never stop growing.** Knowledge is power, and the more you learn, the more confident you'll feel in your business and your abilities.

- **Treat your business like a career, not an experiment.** Dabbling leads to dabbling results. Commit fully, and your business will rise to meet you.

- **Set a clear goal and back it up with daily action.** Be specific about what you want, give it a deadline, and show up every day like your future depends on it ... because it does.

I Dare You to Take Action

I dare you to break the fear cycle.

You've read how fear can hold you back and disguise itself as procrastination, self-doubt, or comfort-zone excuses. Now it's time to break free. I dare you to stop letting fear control your decisions and start taking bold action.

Ask yourself:

- What fears are keeping me stuck in the same place?
- How long am I willing to let fear dictate my future?
- What's one small step I can take right now to face my fear head-on?

You know what fear is costing you—now it's time to act.

Here's your challenge:

Pick one fear you've been avoiding and take immediate action. Don't wait to feel ready. Start now, even if your heart races and your stomach churns.

Remember, fear is just a shadow. Action is the light that chases it away. With every step you take, your confidence grows and fear loses its grip.

I dare you to feel the fear and move anyway. Break the cycle, take the step, and watch yourself get closer to the life you're meant for.

WHEN THE DREAM IS BIG ENOUGH, THE FACTS DON'T COUNT

There are moments in life when you don't have time to second-guess yourself. Moments when hesitation could cost you everything. Moments when you don't care what it takes—you'll figure it out.

I learned this lesson in the hardest way possible.

My daughter, Autumn, started having seizures when she was around five years old. At first, we didn't know what they were. We thought maybe she was clearing her throat in her sleep. Little sounds, little things you could brush off—until you couldn't.

One morning, she woke up, her little voice shaky, saying, "Mommy, my heart is beeping funny." Then her whole body went weak.

I placed my hand on her chest and felt that something was wrong. My husband and I rushed her to the emergency room. What followed was years of unanswered questions, doctor after doctor, test after test—until finally, after pushing, persisting, and refusing to accept "we don't know" as an answer, we got a breakthrough.

Lyme disease.

And the treatment that could actually help her? Insurance wouldn't cover it.

But before we even got to that diagnosis, we had one of the scariest nights of our lives.

One early morning, I happened to be awake before the sun came up. I had a newborn at the time, and I was up late taking care of her, exhausted. I almost went back to bed, but decided instead to start working on something for my daughter's T-ball team. And then, I heard it. That weird sound. The one we had heard before but never fully understood.

I walked into Autumn's room, and what I saw sent my heart into my throat.

Her eyes were open but shifted to the side. Her mouth was making a chewing motion. Her hand was smacking against her chest. Something was wrong. I screamed for my husband. Seconds later, she stopped breathing.

In that moment, there was no time to think—only time to act. My husband immediately started CPR while I was on the phone with 911, my hands shaking, my mind racing. Time slowed down, and all I could do was pray.

By the grace of God, she started breathing again before the paramedics arrived. But that night changed everything. It was the moment I knew we couldn't wait for answers—we had to fight for them.

And when we finally got them?

We were broke. We didn't have extra money lying around. But let me tell you something, when it's your child's life on the line, you don't check your bank account. You find a way.

We took every dollar of our tax return, scraped together whatever we could, and paid for that treatment out of pocket. Because when the dream is big enough, the facts don't count.

And that's exactly what it takes to win in business.

The Truth About Success in Network Marketing

So many people tell me, "I'd love to invest in my business, but I don't have the money."

Let me ask you something: If your child were sick and the only thing standing between them and healing was money, would you find a way?

Of course, you would.

Yet when it comes to our dreams—our family's future, our ability to create financial freedom—we hesitate. We let "I don't have the money" or "I don't have the time" become an excuse. We tell ourselves we'll start later, when things are easier.

But here's what I've learned …

**The people who succeed are the ones
who stop looking at the facts and
start focusing on their dream.**

The fact was, we were broke. Our circumstances said that we had no insurance coverage for what we needed. But the dream?

The dream was my daughter's health. And because the dream was big enough, we found a way.

The same principle applies to building your business.

So, What's Your Dream?

- Is it to get out of debt?
- To bring your spouse home from a job they hate?
- To never have to choose between paying a bill and taking your kids on vacation?
- To finally break free from the cycle of struggle and build real wealth?

Whatever it is, you need to let it burn inside of you so deeply that the facts don't count anymore. Because when your dream is big enough, you stop making excuses.

You figure it out.

Success in this business—and in life—isn't about resources. It's about resourcefulness. It's about how badly you want it. It's about how willing you are to push through obstacles, doubts, and fears.

When the dream is big enough, the facts don't count.

Dream so big that you stop looking at the facts, and start finding a way.

Key Takeaways to WIN

- **If it mattered enough, you'd find a way.** Just like you would for your family—do the same for your dreams.

- **Success isn't about resources—it's about resourcefulness.** It's not what you have, it's what you're willing to do.

- **Big dreams make bold moves.** When your "why" is strong enough, the "how" shows up.

- **Excuses keep you stuck—action sets you free.** Don't wait for perfect. Start messy. Just start.

- **Let your dream be louder than your doubts.** Facts might say "you can't," but your faith says "watch me."

I Dare You to Take Action

I dare you to stop waiting for better circumstances— and start becoming the woman who makes things happen.

1. **Define your nonnegotiable dream**. What's the one thing that, if you accomplished it, would change your life forever? Write it down. Make it real.

2. **Stop letting "facts" hold you back**. Not enough money? Sell something, pick up extra work, cut unnecessary expenses. Not enough time? Wake up an hour earlier, cut out TV, and say no to distractions.

3. **Commit to investing in yourself**. Whether it's a course, coaching, or resources to grow your business, don't let money be the excuse. If you'd find a way to save your child's life, find a way to save your future.

4. **Adopt the "figure it out" mindset**. No one successful had all the answers when they started. They just decided to start and committed to figuring it out as they went.

5. **Take immediate action**. Right now, not tomorrow. Make the call. Send the message, sign up for the thing you've been hesitating on. Do what you've been putting off.

Because if you keep waiting, you'll keep waiting.

But if you move—even if it's messy—you just might change everything.

ATTITUDE IS EVERYTHING

*H*ave you ever noticed how some people just seem to breeze through success, while others are stuck in constant struggle? I know I've observed it many times, and I've come to realize that it's not necessarily about how skilled or talented someone is—it's their attitude that makes all the difference.

Thinking back to when I first got started in direct sales, I had big goals—a drive to succeed—but honestly, my skills were a little rusty. What I didn't realize at the time was that attitude would play a much bigger role in my success than I'd thought. There were times when I felt like I was drowning in self-doubt, but I kept hearing that 95% of success is attitude and only 5% is skill. That really changed my perspective.

I mean, we've all met people who are incredibly skilled, but their attitude? Not so great. It just goes to show that skill alone isn't enough.

It's like they walk into a room and the energy drops faster than a balloon losing air … suddenly, the room feels heavier and the vibe shifts from upbeat to draining. You know the kind. And it's not because they lack ability. It's their mindset.

On the other hand, I've met people who might not have the most talent, but they approach every challenge with such a positive, can-do attitude that you can't help but root for them. The energy they bring is infectious.

The great thing about attitude is that it's not something you're born with—it's a choice—a skill you can work on and grow. I've learned that when negativity starts creeping in, I can choose to focus on the good stuff instead of letting those little setbacks take me down.

Let me tell you a story about my daughter, Kara. She was one of those kids who just never let anything get in her way—a total go-getter. She believed she could do anything! Probably because she was never told she couldn't.

It brings a smile to my face as I think about how independent and determined she was growing up. I'll never forget her freshman year of high school …

She had her heart set on making the softball team, but to make the team, she had to try out, of course. Kara worked her tail off during those tryouts. She gave it everything she had—her energy, her effort, her heart. She had the best attitude on that field, no matter how tough things got. But when the day was said and done, sadly, she didn't make the team.

Now, I'll tell you, I was so proud of her, because instead of letting that defeat her, she went straight up to the coach and said, "Coach, I'll do whatever it takes. I'll be there for the team in any way I can. Can I just practice with the team, even if I can't play in the games? I want to learn and grow and get better."

She wasn't about to just walk away and give up. Her coach agreed! (Sure, he was probably thinking, *Yeah, right … come to practice every day without the chance of playing in the game? Let's see how long that lasts.)*

So, every day, Kara became the first one at practice and the last one to leave. She was always there, always showing up—even though some of the other girls on the team weren't exactly welcoming. They treated her as if she wasn't a part of the team most of the time. But Kara kept her head high, kept her heart in the game, and kept showing up with that same amazing attitude.

And then something incredible happened. *The coach noticed.*

Now, I'm a big believer in this: if you've got someone with a great attitude, you can teach them anything. But if someone's got a bad attitude, no matter how much you try to teach them, they're never going to get it. You've got to have a teachable attitude. You've got to be willing to learn and grow.

And that's exactly what Kara had. She was teachable, coachable, and eager to improve. Within just a few games, not only did she earn an official spot on the team, but she also became a starter!

The raw truth is: your attitude is powerful—you can do everything *right* with the wrong attitude, and fail. But you can do everything *wrong* with the right attitude and succeed beyond your wildest dreams. Just like Kara did.

Developing a Positive Attitude

One of the best tricks I've learned to keep myself in a positive mindset has been to surround myself with uplifting, feel-good content. Whether it's reading motivational books, listening to empowering podcasts, or following people on social media who inspire me, soaking up positive messages can do wonders for reshaping your thinking. I try my best to fill my day with things that uplift me and keep me focused on growth.

I've also learned that what I share online matters. If my feed is full of complaints or negativity, it sends the wrong message to people who might be watching, whether they're team members, customers, or business partners. That energy is contagious!

Now, I've made it a habit to only post things that reflect a positive, growth-focused mindset. It not only lifts me up, but it attracts the kind of people I want to work with. It's amazing how much more opportunity comes your way when you intentionally create that vibe.

But here's the simplest—and most powerful—thing I've incorporated into my life: practicing gratitude. I set aside a few minutes every day to think about the things I'm thankful for, no matter how big or small.

At first, I thought it was just a good thing to do, but over time. I started noticing a shift in my mindset. Instead of focusing on what wasn't working, I started to see what was going right. And that was huge!

The Power of a Positive Attitude

Let's be honest—there are days in this business when your attitude is the only thing holding you together. Maybe the orders aren't coming in like you hoped, or you've heard one too many no's in a row. We've all been there. But over the years, I've learned something simple yet powerful: your mindset *is* your momentum.

I've seen it in my own life more times than I can count. When I choose to stay positive—even when it's hard—I'm able to think clearly, rally my team, and keep moving forward. But when I let discouragement or doubt creep in, it's like trying to run through quicksand. I just get stuck.

I'll never forget one day in particular when that mindset was truly put to the test. It was the very last day of the month, and my unit needed over $16,000 in retail sales *that day* to earn our car—a goal that seemed impossible at the time.

Most people would have looked at that number and thought, *There's no way. How could we possibly do that?* Especially since we had never hit that kind of number before.

But I made a choice. I wasn't going to let the enormity of that goal crush my belief. I decided to stay positive, stretch myself, and stretch my team to do the best we could.

We didn't focus on the impossibility of the number; we focused on what we could control—the energy, the mindset, and the effort we put in that day.

Everyone on the team reached out to their customers and cheered each other on for every sale that was made. We were enrolled in the goal together because of that infectious excitement.

And you know what happened? *We had our biggest day ever.* We surpassed the $16,000 target and finished up way before the cut-off that night. It wasn't magic—it was the result of unwavering belief and maintaining a positive attitude in the face of a really big challenge.

That experience was proof that mindset really does make all the difference. The people who approach challenges with doubt and fear will often hold themselves back, while those who face obstacles with optimism and confidence are the ones who push through and achieve the impossible.

Building a Winning Attitude

Look, it's not always easy to stay positive—especially when things aren't going your way. But I learned that attitude is absolutely something you can choose every day. You can't always control the challenges you face, but you can control how you react to them. And that's where the power lies.

If I could offer one piece of advice to anyone starting out in direct sales, it would be this: focus on your attitude first. Develop it, protect it, and nourish it. Surround yourself with positive influences, practice gratitude, and always choose to look at challenges as opportunities to grow. Once I made that my focus, the rest of my journey became so much easier.

Remember, attitude isn't just about how you think or what you believe, it's also about how you show up. Every day, you have a choice to bring positivity into this world. That choice will shape your journey, and, ultimately, your success.

Key Takeaways to WIN

- **Attitude beats experience.** You don't need to be great to get started; you just need to start. A positive attitude and a willingness to learn will take you a lot further than waiting until you feel "ready." The truth is, skills can be learned, but your *attitude*? That's something you get to choose every single day.

- **Attitude determines success.** You can be the most talented person in the room, but if your mindset is in the gutter, you're going to struggle. Even if you're still figuring things out, a strong, hopeful attitude can carry you far. Most success comes down to your mindset, not just your skill set.

- **Attitude is contagious.** Your energy affects your team, your customers, and even your family. When you show up with belief and excitement, people feel it, and they want to be part of it. A good attitude doesn't just help *you* win, it helps lift everyone around you, too.

I Dare You to Take Action

I dare you to choose your attitude.

You've just read how your attitude can shape your success in business and in life. Now it's time to put that mindset into motion. I dare you to take control of your attitude and choose positivity in every situation you face today.

Ask yourself:

- What mindset will I choose today, no matter what comes my way?
- How can I reframe a current setback as a chance to grow?
- How can I bring more positivity into my daily interactions with customers, team members, or family?

Here's your challenge:

Today, pick one situation where your attitude needs a boost—whether it's an uncomfortable conversation, a difficult task, or a challenging goal—and choose to approach it with positivity.

While you don't always have control over your circumstances, you do get to control how you respond. Focus on the opportunities instead of the obstacles.

I dare you to choose your attitude, protect your peace, and carry that positive energy into everything you do.

FIND YOUR MENTORS

I get myself into some of the most unusual situations while traveling, and it would be easy for me to tell myself that I'm an idiot. Instead, I choose to look at each experience as an adventure, post about it for my community, and laugh at myself both while it's happening and when it's all over.

I'll never forget a leadership event when I was still a new sales director. At that time, I had a massive fear of flying. I mean, if there were a medal for worrying about every possible worst-case scenario in the air, I'd have it hanging on my wall. But I always say, if you really want to conquer that fear, take four flights in five days—and guess what? You get used to it. (It's not fun, but you get used to it.)

On this particular trip, I found myself in the colossal Atlanta, Georgia, airport, trying to juggle my luggage situation like a one-woman circus act. I had my purse slung over one shoulder, a smaller bag for under the seat in front of me, and a roll-away suitcase that was small enough to fit in the overhead bin—but still big enough to cause me all kinds of chaos.

I was rushing through the terminal trying to make it to my gate when the anxiety started to kick in. I hurried down a couple of escalators, and just as I thought I was in the clear, my suitcase decided to take off on its own, nearly taking me out as it tumbled ahead of me on the final escalator.

In that moment, I swear I saw my life flash before my eyes. My heart jumped to my throat, and all I could think was, "This is it. This is how I die—tragically, on an escalator, suitcase in tow." But somehow, thankfully, I managed to recover without the disaster I was sure was imminent.

Just as I was trying to catch my breath, a sweet, calm voice broke through my panic. "Hey, honey, if you'd like, you can use the service elevator," an airport employee called out, flashing me a reassuring smile.

"Oh, thank you!" I thought, *Finally, a break!* So, I made my way to the elevator, ready for some smooth sailing—until I realized I didn't know the code to access it. My brain, in full-on panic mode, went blank. I tried to keep my cool, but inside I was like, *What now?*

As I stood there, awkwardly fumbling around, a kind stranger came up, swiped a badge, and voilà—the elevator doors opened. I stepped in only to find myself surrounded by a bunch of pilots and flight attendants. *Wait a second,* I thought, glancing down at my navy blue suit.

It suddenly clicked—our company's leadership uniform that year was navy blue, and OMG, this woman had mistaken me for a stewardess! You've got to be kidding me.

Before I knew it, I was whisked away in a service elevator for airport employees only, descending into the depths of the airport like some sort of secret agent—but not the cool kind.

The doors opened to a bustling cargo area, suitcases zooming by on conveyor belts, and I was completely lost. Alone. Separated from my friend. *Keep it together, Susan*, I thought.

Needless to say, I was flustered, panicked, and a little bit like a chicken running around with its head cut off. But I couldn't let that stop me. So I took a deep breath and, in true "I'm not giving up" fashion, I navigated through a maze of subway trains, finally finding my way back to the terminal—barely in time for my flight.

When You Need More Than Just Determination

Looking back at that chaotic experience, I realized something profound: determination got me to my gate, but a mentor or guide would have gotten me there without the drama. This experience taught me an invaluable lesson about the power of guidance that I now apply to every area of my life.

Have you ever asked for advice from someone and instantly regretted it? Yeah, me too! That day at the airport, I was getting "help" from well-meaning strangers who didn't actually know where I needed to go. While the employee thought she was offering a helpful shortcut, she actually sent me straight into confusion.

It's a perfect metaphor for what happens in business and life when we take advice from the wrong sources. Just as I wouldn't want navigation help from someone who doesn't know my destination, I've learned not to take business advice from those who haven't achieved what I'm aiming for.

The Power of Experienced Guidance

Think about how different my experience would have been if I'd had an experienced traveler by my side that day—someone who knew exactly which paths to take and how to navigate efficiently. No panic, no detours, no near-disasters.

That's what a true mentor does in your life and business. They've walked the path before you. They know the pitfalls, the short-cuts that work, and the ones that lead you astray when you need to be moving forward.

When I first started in direct sales, I was like a sponge. I was hungry to learn, not just to improve myself but also to create a better life for my family. I knew I was teachable, coachable, and willing to learn! But I needed to be intentional about whose guidance I followed.

I started asking myself: Are they where I want to be in life? Can they help me grow? Do they have a strong track record, or are they new to my industry?

The Mentor Who Changed Everything

One of those incredible people was my dear friend and mentor, Tammy West-Murrian. She was always there, encouraging me, lifting me up, and helping me become a better version of myself.

I remember one night, after an event, feeling completely defeated and overwhelmed. I so badly wanted to move up in my business, but everything seemed insurmountable. Tammy was there, patiently listening, encouraging me, and reminding me that I was capable of so much more. Over the years, her wisdom and support have been a constant source of strength.

Having someone like Tammy in my life has made all the differ-ence. She has been my guide—someone who had successfully navigated the challenges I was still struggling to understand. She showed me where the opportunities were and which pitfalls to avoid.

When Determination Meets Direction

My adventures have shown me I have determination—I'm going to reach my goals no matter what obstacles appear. But imagine combining that determination with proper direction! That's the unbeatable combination that mentorship provides.

Sometimes, we hold ourselves back because we're afraid to invest in mentorship or coaching. But one of the best decisions I ever made was investing in a coach—someone who actually knew where I wanted to go and the best way to get there.

It's great to surround yourself with successful people, but sometimes, you need someone who has been there and has nothing to gain or lose from your success. A coach is there to help you map out a plan, hold you accountable, and make sure you're doing the things that stretch you.

Working with a coach completely changed my perspective. It helped me grow in ways I didn't think were possible. Without that guidance, I'm not sure I would have ever built Women Wired to Win. This brand came to life after years of thought, self-reflection, and growth. It wasn't something that happened quickly—it took about eight years to finally realize that I had a story worth sharing.

How to Find Your Mentor or Guide

Alright, let's get real about finding mentors, because we already know how crucial it is to have someone who has been there, done that, and can show us the ropes.

Here's how you can start connecting with the right people:

Go to events. If there's a conference, seminar, or training event in your area, go. Seriously, those are golden opportunities to meet people who are crushing it in the industry. Don't be shy—introduce yourself, start a conversation, and get to know them. You never know where those connections could lead.

Use social media. I know it sounds simple, but platforms like Facebook groups, LinkedIn, or even Instagram can be a goldmine for finding mentors. Look for people who inspire you, send them a message, and let them know you'd love to learn from them. Just be respectful of their time—it goes a long way.

Seek recommendations. Don't be afraid to ask your network for recommendations. Maybe someone you know has worked with a great mentor or coach and can connect you. Building your circle is key, and sometimes those personal referrals can make all the difference.

Don't Go Alone

That experience in Atlanta was uncomfortable. It was embarrassing, even. But you know what? I didn't let it break me. Instead, I laughed at myself and pushed through the mess. The fear didn't go away, but I did it—because sometimes, when your dream is big enough, the fear becomes background noise, and you move forward anyway.

Now imagine that same determination, but with a mentor who knows exactly which steps to take and which to avoid. That's the transformative power of finding the right guide.

For all the direct sellers and network marketers reading this, let me tell you, I get it. You've probably had your own moments of feeling completely lost and confused.

Maybe you've had a Facebook post go totally wrong, or you've shown up to a virtual meeting and felt like no one's really listening to you. Maybe you've reached out to someone you've been dying to work with, only to get crickets in response. That's a real thing.

The fear of rejection, the awkward moments, the self-doubt … it all shows up. But here's what I want you to hear: it's part of the ride. And with the right mentor by your side, you'll navigate it all with more grace and confidence than I had during my chaotic journey that day in the airport.

Remember, when you find the right mentors and coaches—whether it's someone who's already achieved what you desire or a coach who can help you reach the next level—your journey becomes a lot clearer.

You don't have to do it alone. You don't have to end up lost when you're trying to reach your destination. Find someone who can challenge, inspire, and guide you. They'll help you see things in a new light and show you that there are still heights you're capable of reaching—without all the unnecessary drama and detours.

Key Takeaways to WIN

- **Hustle is great, but guidance gets you there faster.** Determination matters, but direction from the right mentor is what keeps you out of the chaos.

- **Don't take advice from people who haven't done what you're trying to do.** If they haven't built it, they can't help you build it.

- **Mentors help you grow with less stress and more confidence.**

  They know the shortcuts that work—and the ones to avoid.

- **It's okay to laugh at yourself.** Life can get chaotic, and things might not go as planned. Embrace the awkward moments, laugh it off, and remember that it's all part of the adventure.

- **Keep moving forward, even when you feel lost.** Whether you're navigating a crowded airport or a tough day in your business, keep moving. It's not about being perfect—it's about taking the next step.

I Dare You to Take Action

I dare you to find your guide.

You've just read how mentorship can turn chaos into clarity and how the right guide can change the outcome in a huge way! Now it's your turn to act.

Ask yourself:

- Who in my life or industry inspires me and could be a mentor?
- Am I truly coachable, or am I trying to figure everything out by myself?
- What's one area of my business where I need clearer direction?

Once you have your answers, take action.

Here's your challenge:

Reach out to one person you admire in your business and introduce yourself or ask one thoughtful question. Or, if you're ready, explore hiring a coach who can guide your next steps.

Remember, determination will take you far, but aligned direction gets you there faster and with far less stress.

I dare you to stop trying to do it all alone and start seeking guidance that helps you grow with more direction and confidence.

YOUR INNER CIRCLE MATTERS

"You become like the people you spend the most time with."

We hear it all the time, but do we really believe it? Think about it—have you ever noticed how close-knit friend groups start to sound the same, act the same, even think the same? It's not a coincidence. Your core group naturally rubs off on you.

I'm not saying you should try to be like everyone else, but I am saying that who you surround yourself with *matters*—not just emotionally, but mentally, physically, and spiritually. Your circle influences the way you think, the way you see yourself, and even what you believe is possible for your life.

I didn't always understand this. But looking back, I can see how the people in my life shaped my path—sometimes for the better, sometimes … not so much.

A New Town, a New Reality

My husband and I were just 21 when we moved to Milton, Delaware, with our two little girls. Money was tight, as usual, and we were hustling, trying to make things work. I had picked up a part-time job at Ann Taylor Loft, and that's where I met someone who would unknowingly introduce us to a world that would change our lives forever.

She and her husband were involved in a network marketing business, and before we knew it, we weren't just learning about a business opportunity—we were learning about **personal growth, mindset, and influence.**

This was the first time I really started to understand the power of association. The more time we spent around these people, the more our perspective shifted. They talked about vision, belief, and possibilities. They spoke life into us. And because we were around them, we started to think differently.

I didn't realize it then, but this shift in mindset was preparing me for something much bigger—a storm I never saw coming.

The Wake-Up Call That Changed Everything

It started with a sore throat.

Just a normal, nagging sore throat that wouldn't go away. Because we were new in town, I had to find a new doctor. So, I scheduled an appointment, expecting nothing more than a prescription for antibiotics.

But since I was a new patient, the doctor suggested a full physical, including a Pap smear, which I was about six months overdue for. I thought nothing of it at the time.

A few days later, my phone rang. The nurse on the other end said, "The doctor would like to discuss your results with you and your husband."

Instantly, my heart sank. I knew this wasn't just about a sore throat.

When we finally spoke with the doctor, the news hit like a ton of bricks: severe abnormalities. **Stage zero cervical cancer.**

I was stunned. I had no symptoms. No signs. Just 18 months before, everything had been normal. Now, suddenly, I was facing a reality I wasn't prepared for.

Fear tried to take over. What if it was worse than they thought? What if it had spread? What about my babies? My husband? My mind raced through every worst-case scenario.

But in that moment, the strength of my *inner circle* became real.

The Strength of Your Circle

Because of the people we had surrounded ourselves with—people of faith, people who spoke life instead of fear—I was not alone in this. My new community rallied around me, praying over me, speaking words of healing and faith. They reminded me that God had a plan, even in the middle of my fear.

I went through the necessary procedures, including a biopsy and surgery. The doctors warned me that I might struggle with future pregnancies due to an incompetent cervix. But let me tell you—**God is bigger than medical predictions.**

Not only was I completely healed, but later, when I went for follow-up visits, my doctor was stunned. No cancer. No scar tissue. Nothing.

She even said, "I don't know how to explain this."

But I did.

It was **God**. And it was also the people He had placed in my life at just the right time—people who encouraged me, lifted me up, and strengthened my faith when I was too weak to stand on my own.

Evaluating Your Circle

Think about the people you spend the most time with—how do they make you feel?

- Encouraged?
- Inspired?
- Motivated to go after your goals?

Or do they leave you feeling:

- Doubtful?
- Drained?
- Stressed out?

Over the years, after coaching thousands of women in business, I've noticed a pattern. Whenever I ask, "What's holding you back?" the answer almost always points to someone close to them—a spouse, a friend, a family member—who isn't exactly cheering them on.

Maybe it's little jokes about their "side hustle." Maybe it's a sarcastic, *"Oh, you're still doing that thing?"* Those little digs add up. Before you know it, you're second-guessing yourself. You start hearing their doubt in your own head.

It's like trying to run a race with ankle weights. You can do it, but dang, it's a lot harder when the people around you don't believe in you.

Recognizing and Handling Toxic Relationships

What's wild is that the more you surround yourself with people who genuinely believe in you, the more clearly you start noticing the toxic ones.

Sometimes, the toughest relationships to navigate are the ones closest to us. What if the person bringing you down is your spouse? A close friend? A family member?

I won't sugarcoat it—that's tough. But the reality is, *you must find a support system.*

If a relationship constantly brings stress or doubt, it's time to rethink it. Protecting your peace and growth isn't selfish—it's necessary. That doesn't mean cutting out everyone who challenges you—growth comes from being pushed outside your comfort zone. But there's a big difference between someone pushing you to be better and someone making you feel like you'll never be enough.

Be intentional about who gets the most access to your energy—prioritize the ones who challenge you in a way that fuels your growth, not your self-doubt. You need voices that lift you up, not pull you down.

I'm not a professional by any stretch of the imagination, but if you're in a physically or emotionally abusive relationship, **you need to get out.** It's not worth staying in an environment where your safety and well-being are at risk. Please reach out to a professional or a support system if you need help.

There's always support available, and you deserve to be in a safe relationship that lifts you up, not one that abuses you.

Protecting your peace and growth isn't selfish, it's necessary.

If you're in the U.S. and need immediate support, you can call the **National Domestic Violence Hotline at 1-800-799-SAFE (7233)** or visit thehotline.org to chat with someone 24/7.

Find Your Support System

When I think about the most successful people I've coached, one thing is super clear: **It was never just about having the best skills or strategies.**

The real difference? *The people in their corner.*

- The spouse who cheered them on when they doubted themselves.
- The mentor who saw their potential before they even did.
- The friend who reminded them of why they started on the days they wanted to quit.

Your circle matters more than you think. When you surround yourself with people who believe in you and your dreams, everything starts to shift. You see yourself differently. You start believing bigger.

Choose Your Circle Wisely

Remember, you become like the five people you spend the most time with.

So, take a minute to ask yourself who's in your circle.

- Are they pushing you forward or holding you back?
- Are they challenging you to grow or keeping you stuck?

If someone is constantly bringing you down, maybe it's time to put some space between you. That doesn't mean you have to cut them off forever. But sometimes, the best thing you can do—for you and for them—is to take a step back.

You can *love people from a distance* while still protecting your peace, happiness, and growth.

Here's something else to think about—**you're part of someone else's five, too.**

Be the kind of person who lifts others up, speaks life into them, and helps them believe in themselves. Because the more you pour into others, the more it comes back to you.

Choose your circle wisely. In the end, the people you surround yourself with won't just influence your success—*they'll shape the person you become.*

Key Takeaways to WIN

- **The people you spend the most time with can influence how you think and feel about yourself.** Make sure they're people who support your goals and uplift you.

- **Evaluate your relationships** and be honest with yourself—are they helping you grow or holding you back?

- **Don't just look at your inner circle**—think about your online circle, too. Is your social media filled with positivity and people who inspire you?

- **Surround yourself with people who inspire and challenge you.** These are the people who will help you grow and reach your goals.

- **If the people closest to you aren't supportive, find others who can be your support system**—whether that's a mentor, a friend, or a support group.

- **If you're in an abusive relationship, find a way out.** Your safety and well-being come first, and you deserve to be in a supportive relationship.

I Dare You to Take Action

I dare you to evaluate your circle.

You've learned that the people around you influence your life, for better or worse. Now it's time to take action. I dare you to stop letting toxic relationships drain your energy and start choosing people who lift you up and support your dreams.

Ask yourself:

- Who am I spending the most time with, and how do they make me feel?
- Are they helping me grow or holding me back?
- Which relationships inspire me, and which ones leave me drained?

Once you identify which relationships need attention, start making changes. Set boundaries, limit time with negative influences, or distance yourself from people who aren't supportive of your goals. Protect your energy and your peace.

Here's your challenge:

Look closely at your inner circle this week. Reach out to someone who encourages you and let them know you appreciate their support. Then take one step to create distance from a negative influence, whether that's in person or online.

You don't have to walk this journey alone. The right people will help you grow and succeed. Evaluate your circle, choose wisely, and build a support system that moves you toward your dreams.

GOLDEN RULE SERVICE

This business is beautiful … and also kind of bananas.

One minute you're celebrating a team win, the next you find out someone slid into your customer's DMs offering a "better deal" and you lost the sale. Or a prospect you've been nurturing for weeks ghosts you … only to pop up enrolled under someone else.

Cue the deep sigh and the "what just happened?" face.

That's when the Golden Rule gets tested—when your character shows up and speaks louder than your words.

It's easy to talk about doing the right thing when everything's going your way.

But what about when it costs you a sale? Or a team member? Or a promotion?

In this industry, relationships are everything, and integrity matters more than ever.

Just Because You Can Doesn't Mean You Should

In my former direct sales company, we had something called the "Go-Give" mentality—basically, a Golden Rule for how we treated each other, especially when it came to customers and prospects.

The principle was simple: **you don't sell to or recruit someone else's customer or prospect.**

Yes, technically, it's always their choice. But we understood that most people outside the industry don't grasp how it works.

Customers bounce between reps without thinking much about it. Prospects make decisions without knowing the full impact.

That's why it's up to us—the ones who *do* know—to lead with integrity within our company and our organization.

I took that seriously. Like, *seriously* seriously.

If I knew someone was already working with a consultant—even if they had sat out for a while—I almost always made it a point to send them back. Because at the end of the day, it's not just about what you *can* do; it's about what's *right*.

As the saying goes, "Just because you can, doesn't mean you should."

The Time I Could Have Recruited Her—But Didn't

Several years ago, I got a phone call from a woman who found me through my company's website.

We had a great conversation, and I could tell she was already familiar with the company and products—a little too familiar, actually.

So, I leaned in a little more. Asked a few important questions like:

"Have you ever worked with a consultant before?"

"How long ago was that?"

"How was your experience?"

Turns out, she had been a consultant a few *years* earlier. She'd stepped away after suffering a heartbreaking miscarriage of twins at 24 weeks.

Building a business had understandably been the last thing on her mind.

But now, she was ready to give it another go—but the only problem? She couldn't remember the name of her previous sponsor or unit leader.

Technically, I could have enrolled her right then and there. Even customer service told me it was fair game. But it just didn't feel right to me.

So, I asked her for the info I'd need to look into her past enrollment, and I made a call to the company. After some digging, I found her former sponsor. Not only that—come to find out, it was someone I knew personally from a sister unit in our area.

I called her and said something like, "You're not going to believe this, but someone from your past team is ready to come back. She didn't remember your name, but I was able to track her back to you after a call to the company. I wanted to make sure she landed back where she belongs."

She was stunned. And extremely grateful.

But to me, it wasn't even a question. I just kept thinking: *What would I want someone to do if the roles were reversed?*

And the wild part? That wasn't the only time.

That same month, I ended up sending *three* different women back to their original recruiters for completely different reasons.

Each one was a moment where I could've chosen what was easy … but instead, I chose what was right. (*I think I passed the test.*)

And you know what happened next?

That same month ended up being my *highest month ever in personal recruits (12) and commission.* (Up to that point anyway.)

Total God moment. Because when you lead with integrity, abundance follows.

Maybe not always in the exact moment, but always in the long run.

The Golden Rule in Action

Treat others how you want to be treated—isn't just a sweet little quote you hang on your wall.

It's a biblical principle to build our life on and a compass for how to do things the right way.

In business it looks like this:

- Referring customers back to their original consultant (even when it stings)

- Cheering on someone else's win
- Choosing what's right over what's easy

Like Zig Ziglar said: *"Live your life in such a way that if someone were to speak badly of you, no one would believe it."*

That's the kind of culture I want to build—one based on trust, character, and doing the right thing even when no one's watching.

Because when you lead with integrity, people *notice*. They trust you. And that's priceless.

Create Wow-Worthy Moments

Success in this business usually comes down to how well you connect with people.

They may not remember everything you said, but they will remember how you made them feel!

Ask yourself: *"After working with me, does my customer feel valued?"*

Make it personal:

- a thank-you note
- a quick check-in
- a surprise sample or gift

Small things go a long way. These touches stick. They make people remember you and tell their friends.

Get to know your people. Ask about their life, not just their order. Celebrate their wins. Check in when they've gone quiet. That's how loyalty with clients—and team culture—gets built.

Listen Actively

When a customer's sharing something with you, give them your full attention. Put your phone down, look them in the eye, and really listen.

Ask questions to clarify their needs and let them know you hear them. A little "I get it" can make someone feel truly seen.

Communicate with Heart and Honesty

Keep your people in the loop. If something's delayed, just let them know. A quick message and a "Thanks for your patience" is all it takes.

And when things go sideways (because they will), take a deep breath, don't overthink it, and just be real.

Put yourself in their shoes and handle it the way *you'd* want someone to handle it for you.

You don't have to be perfect. Just honest. That's what builds trust.

Use the 2+2+2 Follow-Up System

- **2 days** after the purchase: A quick call or text to thank them. Let them know when they can expect their order. Ask for referrals—no shame in that game!
- **2 weeks** later: Check in, answer questions. Offer something new.
- **2 months** later: Suggest a refill or new product. Ask for a testimonial or even offer your business opportunity.

It's not about hounding—it's about *honoring* the relationship.

Handle Conflicts with Class

If a customer or prospect ends up working with someone else, **bless and release.** If someone messages one of "your" people, take the high road and talk it out if you need to, but don't let one moment of offense take you out of your calling.

Golden Rule = Solid Gold Business

Your reputation is your brand. When you're known for doing the right thing—even when no one's watching—people notice, trust you, refer others to you, and stick around. So the next time you're faced with a choice, ask yourself: "If the roles were reversed, how would *I* want to be treated?" Then go do that, because those little touches of care lead to big, lasting results.

Key Takeaways to WIN

- **Treat people like people, not paychecks.** This makes customers feel valued and heard, turning them into loyal supporters who spread the word!

- **Honor your fellow consultants.** Always send people back to the person they were working with when it makes sense to do so.

- **Serve with integrity,** not insecurity. Your reputation is the most valuable product you sell.

- **Do the right thing** even when it's inconvenient—and especially when no one's looking.

  The Golden Rule is not just a principle, it's a strategy for success.

I Dare You to Take Action

I dare you to serve with excellence.

I dare you to take everything you just read and put it into practice. Not someday. Not when it's easy. But *this week*.

Pick one customer and surprise them.

- Send a handwritten note.
- Add an extra gift to their order.
- Check in when they're not expecting it.

If an opportunity comes up to do the right thing when no one else would, take it. While your paycheck comes from the company, your reputation is built on your actions.

Lead with the Golden Rule.

Go the extra mile.

Transform your business, your relationships, and your legacy.

WINNING AT FIRST IMPRESSIONS

*L*et's face it—first impressions matter. Whether we like it or not, people form opinions about who you are and what you're about within seconds of meeting you. Those impressions can stick, so it's crucial to make sure you're sending the right signals.

I learned this lesson firsthand in my career. And let me tell you, it wasn't glamorous.

The Van That Didn't Define Me

At the time, I had just become a new Sales Director and was working toward earning my company car. But behind the scenes, my reality was far from polished. My husband, a painting contractor, had a work van that was badly damaged from an accident. It was our only working vehicle, and we couldn't afford to get it fixed.

So, here I was—dressing like a top-level Sales Director but being dropped off at events in a beat-up, smashed-in van. When my events were at places like the beautiful Embassy Suites, I made a point to have my husband drop me off at the back entrance, far from the main doors.

It wasn't that I was ashamed of our van or my circumstances, I was simply aware that first impressions matter. I understood that the women I was presenting to had an idea of what a successful Sales Director looked like, acted like, and yes, even drove. My intention wasn't to be fake; it was to align with their vision and not create any distractions that might derail their hopes and dreams.

One night, I drove the van myself to an event and parked it far in the back. A fellow Sales Director noticed and approached me. She said, "I admire you so much for not letting anything stop you."

She had no idea the intention behind my actions. But her words shifted something in me. I realized that my image wasn't about hiding my challenges—it was about embodying who I was becoming, not where I was.

Dress for Where You're Going, Not Where You Are

That experience taught me something powerful: your image should reflect your potential, not your present circumstances. I didn't have the perfect car or the ideal situation, but I knew I could control one thing—how I showed up. I made sure my appearance and attitude represented the top leader I was becoming, not the struggling woman driving a broken van.

And guess what? People didn't see the van—they saw my confidence. They saw my professionalism. They saw the vision I was building. That's when I learned a key lesson: you have to dress for where you're going, not where you are.

Stop waiting until you've "arrived" to start looking and acting like the successful version of yourself. When you show up as your future self, dressed for the success you want, it sends a powerful message to everyone around you, including yourself.

The Power of Perception

Believe it or not, people form an impression of you in about seven seconds. That's right, seven seconds! Whether you're walking into a room, hopping on a Zoom call, or showing up to a networking event, people are subconsciously deciding how seriously they'll take you based on how you present yourself.

Imagine walking into a room and seeing two people. One is polished, put-together, and exudes confidence. The other is disheveled, wearing wrinkled clothes, and looks a little scattered.

Without even realizing it, you've already formed an opinion about both of them—who seems more credible, who you'd approach, and who you might want to work with. It's human nature.

That's the power of perception. And as a business owner, you need to own it.

Now, this doesn't mean you need an expensive wardrobe. Trust me, I'm all about thrifting and finding budget-friendly pieces. But it *does* mean you need to be intentional about how you show up. Clean, polished, and confident—because when you look good, you feel good, and that energy will ripple out to everyone around you.

Show Up Like You Mean It

Here's a little exercise I use to keep myself in check: before you leave the house, stand in front of the mirror and ask yourself, "Would I buy from me?" If the answer is no, it's time to make a small adjustment. Freshen up your look, stand tall, and walk with intention.

Even if you're just running to the store, act like you're about to bump into your dream client. When you carry yourself with that level of confidence, opportunities start to open up. You'll get more compliments, you'll make stronger connections, and you'll attract the type of business you've been hoping for.

If it's been a while since you've gotten a compliment about your appearance, consider it a sign—it might be time for a refresh. Whether it's a new hairstyle, a manicure, or just stepping up your wardrobe a bit, those small upgrades can boost your confidence in a big way.

Be a Product of Your Product

Another key element of your image? Be a walking advertisement for what you promote. If you sell skincare, make sure your skin glows. If you sell wellness products, embody that healthy lifestyle. People don't just want to hear you talk about your products—they want to see you living the results and being a reflection of what you're selling. When your image aligns with your message, you build credibility instantly.

In Reflection

Looking back, I realize that beat-up old van was never my story—it was just part of my journey. What mattered most was how I showed up in spite of it. I didn't let my circumstances define me, and neither should you.

Your image is more than just clothes—it's the energy you bring into every room. When you walk in with confidence, like you already belong in the role you're aiming for, you shift how people perceive you. And before long, you'll realize you're no longer pretending to be that successful version of yourself—you've actually become her.

So don't wait. **Show up today like you've already arrived.**

Own your space, your energy, and your future. Because you're not just dressing for where you are—you're dressing for where you're going. And where you're headed? It's big, bold, and beautiful.

Key Takeaways to WIN

- **First impressions matter.** How you present yourself says a lot about you, even before you say a word.

- **Dress for the success you want, not the one you have.** Your image should reflect where you're headed, not just where you are.

- **Don't let your circumstances define you.** People may not know your struggles, but they'll see your determination.

- **Small changes in how you present yourself can make a big difference.** It doesn't have to be expensive, just intentional.

- **Be a product of your product.** It's not just about looking the part—it's about living it.

I Dare You to Take Action

I dare you to show up like you've already arrived.

You've just learned the power of first impressions and how your image can influence the way people perceive you. Now, it's time to take action. I dare you to stop waiting for the perfect circumstances and start showing up as the successful version of yourself right now.

Ask yourself:

- How am I currently presenting myself to others?
- Does my appearance reflect the success I'm working toward?
- What small changes can I make to ensure I'm dressing for the success I want?

So, here's the challenge:

Pick one small change you can make today to improve your image. Whether it's a new hairstyle, a polished outfit, or simply standing tall and owning your space—do it.

Remember, first impressions are powerful. When you dress for where you're going, not where you are, you send a message to the world that you're ready for success. And the best part? You'll start to feel it too.

So, I dare you—show up today like you've already arrived. Own your space, your energy, and your future. People will start to notice, and you'll be amazed at the opportunities that begin to open up.

BE AUTHENTICALLY YOU!

It all started at my daughter's superhero-themed birthday party. Dressed in full superhero attire, I was trying to get a head start on my travel plans to Seminar by checking in for my early morning flight.

When I did, I discovered my "simple" flight had somehow morphed into a *Planes, Trains, and Automobiles* scenario. Yep, you heard that right—a train ride to catch a plane, followed by a car rental to reach the hotel.

Confused much? I know I sure was!

Now, I've been known to be a little, shall we say, "frugal," so I had booked the cheapest flight I could find. Little did I know, that "budget-friendly" choice that popped up on Expedia a few months earlier would turn into the travel debacle of the century.

That night, my family captured the chaos perfectly in a picture: there I was, in full superhero costume—mask, gloves, cape, and all—on the phone with customer service, trying to fix this mess. Definitely not the superhero moment I had imagined. Are you getting a picture of this? (LOL!)

*Yep, that's me dressed as a superhero on hold
with customer service.*

And get this: there was no way to bypass the train station without voiding the rest of my trip. *Say WHAT?!*

In that moment, I had two choices. I could stay frustrated (which, to be honest, was tempting) or turn it into something entertaining. I chose the latter and did what I know best. I made it a story.

I figured, why not take my audience along for the ride? If you know me, you'd expect nothing less than an epic travel tale. From snapping pics at the train station to documenting the hotel room, I shared it all. It was like opening a book of *Where's Waldo?*, but instead, it was *Where's Susan?*

Heck, I even dropped a *Planes, Trains, and Automobiles* movie pic alongside me for good measure. The reaction? Hilarious! My online community loved it. And, believe it or not, my business got a little boost from it, too.

Despite feeling frustrated, flipping the script turned a stressful situation into a memorable journey. And in that moment, I realized how much power there is in just *being yourself*—even when things aren't going according to plan.

Why Being Yourself Matters

Authenticity is the game-changer. It's so easy to hide behind a mask, trying to be someone you think people want to see. But, you don't have to have it all together to make an impact.

People connect with the *real* stuff way more than the polished version.

It's not about being perfect—it's about being honest.

When I started showing up as myself, things got easier. People actually started listening because they could *relate*. And really, who *isn't* a little messy behind the scenes?

That superhero costume I was wearing? It became more than just a costume at a party—it became a perfect symbol for what I was learning in real time: that sometimes life is chaotic, funny, even a little embarrassing. And the meltdown I had? It was 100% human.

All my quirks and imperfections made a bigger impact than any "highlight reel" ever could.

Trying to hide who you are serves no purpose. When you show up authentically, you unlock a whole new level of connection. Trust me, that connection doesn't just strengthen relationships—it opens doors to new opportunities.

To start showing up more authentically, begin with your story. It's the most powerful way to build real connection.

Sharing Your Story—The Ultimate Way to Connect

Each of us has a unique journey, full of incredible wins, devastating losses, and everything in between. It's those real-life moments that help others see who you are and what you're all about.

Putting yourself out there can feel vulnerable. But believe me, it's a superpower. Every one of us has a story to tell. Think about yours—what you've learned, where you've struggled, and how you've overcome challenges. That's not just your story; it's a bridge to connect with others.

For example, when I look back on my journey, I realize that the real turning points didn't happen when everything was perfect—they came when I was willing to be real, trust God, and believe in myself anyway.

It wasn't just about the wins—it was about showing up in the middle of the mess, persevering through the struggles, and staying grounded in who I was created to be.

That's what my story is really about: proof that you can overcome anything when you trust the process, lead with faith, and dare to be fully you.

I could've just shared a post about my business trip and called it a day, but instead, I showed the behind-the-scenes chaos. And people ate it up! I even shared the video of me having a meltdown on the phone with customer service to Facebook—all while still wearing my superhero costume.

Little did I know, my husband was recording the whole thing. It was a priceless moment he couldn't resist. Oh, the irony. Definitely not my most superhero-worthy moment. But one that was totally worth a good laugh!

But here's the thing. It wasn't just "Look at me, I'm a successful entrepreneur"—it was real-life, relatable stuff—messy, honest, and hilarious. And because of that, people felt connected to me.

They weren't just seeing the business side, they were seeing *me*. A real person, doing life with all its crazy moments, just like them.

So next time you think you have to be polished all the time to show up online, think again.

How Does This Help You Build Your Business?

Alright, let's talk business for a sec. You might be thinking, "Okay, being authentic sounds nice and all ... but how does that actually help me grow my biz?"

The simple answer: People are tired of the *perfect, polished* highlight reels that scream, "I have it all together." What people want is connection. They want *you*—the real, honest, messy-in-the-middle version.

And sure, showing up like that takes courage. But remember: *other people's opinions of you are none of your business.* If their opinion doesn't match your purpose, then it doesn't matter.

When you show up authentically, you attract the right people— the ones who vibe with your message, your values, and your story. You're not just building a customer base, you're building a *community*—your people, your tribe.

So, how do you do that?

- **Show up as your true self.** Stop trying to be what you think people want. Share the bloopers, the wins, and yes—even the superhero moments in your life. It'll help people see that you're real and relatable. That's how people connect with you.

- **Tell stories, not just posts.** Don't just show up to sell. Show up to share. Let people in on your journey— the triumphs, the lessons, and the "oops" moments. People want to be inspired by you, so share the full picture. When you open up about the obstacles you've overcome, people can see themselves in your story and think, "Wow, if she can do it, maybe I can too."

Authenticity isn't a strategy—it's a superpower. And when you lead with it, your business naturally grows from a place of connection, not just promotion.

Wrapping It Up

Ultimately, real growth—both in life and business—starts when you embrace who God made you to be, flaws, quirks, and all. When you show up as your true self, you invite the right people, the right opportunities, and the kind of confidence that only comes from knowing you're walking in your purpose.

Your story matters. Your journey matters. And when you share it with boldness, God can use it to inspire and uplift others in ways you may never even realize.

So lean in. Be bold. Be real. Be *you*. The way God wired you wasn't by accident—it was for impact. And when you show up with faith and authenticity, you'll not only overcome fear and judgment … you'll unlock a life and business filled with favor, purpose, and unstoppable growth.

Key Takeaways to WIN

- **Be real and share your story.** When you show up as the real you, people feel it. Your wins, struggles, and "in-the-mess" moments inspire others and create opportunities.

- **Own what makes you different.** Your quirks, strengths, and unique perspective are your advantage. Your energy and confidence appeal to your ideal audience.

- **Grow your business your way.** When you stay true to your values and personality, you naturally attract customers who want to connect with and work with you.

I Dare You to Take Action

I dare you to be authentically *you*.

You've learned how powerful it is to show up as your true self. Now it's time to act.

Ask yourself:

- What parts of me have I been holding back?
- How can I show up more authentically in my business?
- What story do I have that will genuinely connect with my audience?

Don't wait to feel "perfect"—show up as you are. Share your journey, show a behind-the-scenes moment, or be honest about the wins and struggles.

Here's your challenge:

Choose one area of your business where you can be more real this week. Share a story, a moment, or something honest and true.

I dare you to stop hiding behind a mask or trying to fit into a mold. Embrace what makes you unique. Let the real you shine and watch the doors open. Authenticity is your superpower.

WHEN YOU STEP UP,
THE INNER BATTLES SHOW UP

Let's talk about something no one warns you about when you decide to step into entrepreneurship: the mental battles. We've all heard about the hustle, the goals, the big vision. But what no one tells you is how much the *inner* work is going to challenge you along the way.

Trust me, it's real. Once you start moving closer to your dreams, that voice inside your head starts getting louder: *Who do you think you are? Are you even good enough for this? Maybe someone else can do it better.*

I promise you're not alone. We all deal with this chatter in our minds. But I can assure you that *you are enough* just the way you are.

And if you're wondering what that looks like in real life, grab a seat because I have a story for you.

I remember when my girlfriend, Alli Adkins, and I attended Seminar, our company's annual year-end event. We were rooming together (which is a whole different story of laughter and chaos), and we both had our new director dresses ready to go.

Now, let me set the scene: Alli is about six feet tall, and I'm 5'2". We're basically the opposite of each other. But like every Seminar year, we were both excited to finally break out our new director dresses.

So there we were all week, rocking our new dresses and feeling like total boss babes. Everything was great—until I got home. I noticed when I put on that same director dress for my weekly success events, something was … off.

It just didn't fit right. It felt too big, but I shrugged it off and made it work. I started using rubber bands to scrunch it up underneath and adjust it because it seemed longer. But, honestly, I didn't think much of it. After all, I had just worn it all week at Seminar, so it must've been fine.

Fast forward six months later and I'm still wearing this dress, still wrestling with it every time I put it on.

But then something funny happened.

We went to our mid-year leadership event, and when I went to grab my dress from the closet, it wasn't there.

This time, Alli and I weren't rooming together. So when I went looking for my extra-small, petite director dress in the lineup of dresses in the closet, it was missing.

At first I thought, *That's weird …*

Then it clicked.

I picked up the hotel phone, called Alli's room, and said, "Hey girl, can you check the tag on the dress you brought with you?"

You see, in all those months back home, neither of us had bothered to do one very simple thing.

We never checked the tag.

She had grabbed my petite extra-small. And I had grabbed her regular small.

For six months, she'd been stuffed into her dress like a sardine, and I'd been swimming in mine.

Suddenly, everything made sense.

We laughed so hard, because seriously … *How did we not figure this out sooner?*

So often, we try to fit into roles, expectations, or even mind-sets that don't belong to us. Just like I was trying to wear a dress that wasn't made for my body and Alli was uncomfortable in a dress that wasn't her size, a lot of us are walking around uncomfortable in the "role" we think we *should* be playing.

We're trying to wear someone else's success or fit into a mold that wasn't designed for us. And let me tell you, that doesn't work.

When you step up and decide to take action in your business, I can practically guarantee you're going to have self-limiting thoughts. *This doesn't feel quite right. Maybe I'm not cut out for this. This role should be filled by someone else.*

Believe it or not, those thoughts are normal. I would even argue that if you're feeling like the shoes don't fit (or the dress, in my case!), it means you're on the right path. Those feelings don't show up when you're sitting back and staying comfortable—they show up when you're pushing yourself, stepping into new territory, and going after things that are bigger than what you've done before.

So, what can you do when the voice in your head is telling you that you're not enough?

1. Acknowledge it.
The first step is recognizing it for what it is. When that voice pops up and tells you, "Who do you think you are?"—acknowledge it. The more you recognize it, the less power it has over you. Try saying something like, "Thanks for trying to keep me safe. I'm doing something new, and I know it feels scary, but I promise it's going to be worth it."

2. Reconnect with your "why."
Remember why you started this journey. Was it to provide for your family? Was it to have more freedom? Maybe it was to create something you can be proud of. Focus on that. When you remember your deeper purpose, that voice of doubt starts to fade.

3. Celebrate your progress.
Self-doubt thrives when you forget to celebrate your wins. Big or small, every step forward counts. Look at where you are now compared to where you started, and give yourself some credit!

4. Be yourself.
You don't need to wear someone else's dress. There's only one you, and that's who your business needs. You're not meant to play a part that doesn't fit. Trying to squeeze into a role that isn't yours will only leave you feeling like a fraud.

Instead, lead with your true, authentic self—and trust me, that's more than enough.

Beating Burnout

Burnout is a sneaky beast. It creeps in slowly. At first, you're excited and ready to tackle everything, working late into the night and checking things off your list.

But somewhere along the way, you forget to pause, recharge, and take care of yourself. Before you know it, you're running on fumes. You start to feel overwhelmed, and soon enough, you're burned out. I've been there too, and let me tell you, it's not pretty.

So, what can you do?

1. **Set boundaries.** In the hustle of building your business, it's easy to forget the importance of personal time. Make sure you're blocking out time for self-care—whether it's exercising, spending time with family, or simply unplugging from work. This is a must! Even God modeled this for us: "And on the seventh day God finished his work that he had done, and he rested on the seventh day from all his work" (Genesis 2:2 ESV). If God took a day to rest, so should we. Rest isn't optional—it's part of the plan.

2. **Create a sustainable routine.** Success doesn't come from working yourself into the ground. It comes from consistency. Break down your goals into smaller, more manageable chunks, and create a daily routine that doesn't leave you feeling drained.

3. **Ask for help.** This is a big one. A lot of entrepreneurs struggle with this, especially in network marketing. There's a mindset that we need to do everything ourselves. But it's okay to ask for help. Whether it's from your mentor, your team, or a friend, you don't have to do it alone. You need people to lean on.

Remember, you can't pour from an empty cup. Taking care of yourself is just as important as taking care of your business.

Turning Rejection into Growth

Let's talk about rejection. It's tough, right? Whether it's a potential client saying "no," a team member quitting, or someone just not being interested, rejection can feel personal. But here's what I've learned over the years: **rejection is not a reflection of your worth,** but it is part of the process.

When I first started out, I took every "no" so personally. I thought it meant I wasn't good enough or that my business wasn't worth anyone's time. But what I came to understand was that every rejection was an opportunity for growth. Instead of letting it shake your confidence, use it to strengthen your approach.

Here's how:

1. **Separate yourself from the outcome.** A "no" doesn't mean you're not good enough—it just means the person you spoke to wasn't ready yet. It's about them, not you. Focus on the process, not just the result.

2. **Practice resilience.** Every "no" gets you closer to a "yes." It's a numbers game. The more people you reach

out to, the more likely you are to find the ones who are a perfect fit. I've learned that if you keep going, the right people will come along.

3. **Learn from it.** Take a moment after each rejection to reflect. Was there something I could do differently next time? Don't take rejection personally—take it as a lesson.

You're Bigger Than Your Battles

I've been through it all—self-doubt, burnout, rejection—and I'm telling you: you are not alone. Entrepreneurship is tough but *you are tougher.* When you step up to play big, that inner battle *will* show up. It might come in the form of doubt, exhaustion, or fear of failure. But these struggles don't mean you're on the wrong path—they mean you're pushing boundaries and growing.

Whatever challenge you're facing, know this: you have everything you need inside you to rise above it. Use the tools I've shared to navigate the mental hurdles when they appear. Don't let them hold you back. Let them fuel you.

Every obstacle is a stepping stone. Every moment of resistance is a chance to become stronger. Keep your head up, your heart strong, and show up as your best, most authentic self. Because that's exactly what your business needs.

Your success is already inside you—and it's just around the corner.

Now, let's do the work.

Key Takeaways to WIN

- **Self-doubt is normal.** Everyone feels it, but it only has power if you let it stop you.

- **You are enough.** Stop trying to wear someone else's dress. Be yourself. You attract more people that way.

- **Celebrate your wins.** Big and small, every step forward is progress.

- **Rise above the struggles.** Treat mental hurdles as a chance to grow. Keep going, you're stronger than you think.

I Dare You to Take Action

I dare you to rise above.

You've learned about the challenges that come with stepping up in your business—self-doubt, burnout, rejection. These are real battles that can shake your confidence and slow your momentum. Now it's time to act.

Ask yourself:

- What mental roadblocks are keeping me from going all in?
- How can I reframe rejection to build resilience?
- What habits will help me prevent burnout and stay energized?

Don't let these battles hold you back. Every time you face one and rise above it, you grow stronger and step closer to your goals.

Here's your challenge:

Choose one internal struggle you're facing—self-doubt, exhaustion, or rejection—and turn it into a stepping stone. Acknowledge it, reconnect with your why, and take one action today that moves you forward.

I dare you to face those inner battles head-on and use them as fuel for growth. You're tougher than you think, and every challenge is an opportunity to build strength. Take control of your mindset and turn your inner battles into the fuel that drives your success.

YOUR PAST DOES NOT DEFINE YOU

I wish I could tell you that my upbringing was peaceful and easy, but that wouldn't be the truth. Now, before I share some deeply personal experiences, I want you to know that every family story is complex, layered with love, pain, growth, and grace. We all struggle with invisible pressure.

My mom, like many of us, faced challenges that I can only suspect—from what she's shared—came from unhealed wounds of her own childhood. These challenges were not always easy to navigate, and they affected how she interacted with us.

The woman in these stories was fighting internal battles I couldn't fully understand as I was growing up. Generational patterns and life's overwhelming demands can push any of us to our breaking point.

I share these experiences not to cast blame or define anyone by their worst moments, but because they shaped my understanding of resilience, forgiveness, and the power of rewriting our stories. These difficulties became the foundation for profound healing—not just for me, but for our entire family.

We are all capable of both tremendous love and unintentional harm. We all have moments we wish we could go back and handle differently. The gift of time, healing, and grace has allowed our family relationships to evolve and grow in beautiful ways that once seemed hard to imagine.

As you read these stories, please remember that they represent seasons of struggle, not the entirety of anyone's character. They are shared with love, respect, and the hope that vulnerability can create connection and healing for others walking similar paths. As the saying goes, "Be kind, for everyone you meet is fighting a hard battle."

The Car Accident

The day started just like any other. I wanted to go play at a friend's house, but I needed a ride. I remember my mom was working in the front yard and I felt nervous about asking her.

As a middle school girl, I was probably being selfish, wanting what I wanted, but should I really have been so afraid to ask? Regardless, I asked her anyway, and she seemed super annoyed but agreed to take me, albeit hesitantly. A few minutes later, we were in the car, heading down the familiar back roads to my best friend's house.

Looking out the window, I could see the sky darkening, clouds gathering like a warning sign; it appeared a storm was coming. Little did I know what kind of storm it would be.

During the ride, I could feel my mom's displeasure growing. She wasn't happy about stopping what she was doing to take me, and as the minutes ticked by, her frustration became increasingly apparent.

Suddenly, years of suppressed pain erupted. She began venting about everything she'd been carrying from her past—a release that had been building for who knows how long.

In these moments, the weight of her unhealed trauma seemed to take over, transforming the mother I knew into someone driven by pain rather than love. I could feel my heart racing in my chest. By this time, the rain was coming down heavily, splattering against the windows, mirroring the tension in the air.

I remember sitting in the front seat, begging her to *please* slow down.

But she did the exact opposite.

Gripping the steering wheel, her knuckles white with anger, she pushed even harder on the gas.

The next thing I knew, we were swerving off the road, and the car began flipping over and over. I had been sitting in the front passenger seat, unbuckled, and I'll never forget the sickening thud of my head slamming into the ceiling as we flipped.

Everything spun wildly out of control.

The ceiling above me seemed to collapse in an instant, only to stretch back up, then collapse again—like a never-ending nightmare. The world felt like it was being torn apart.

Finally, after what seemed like forever, the car came to a stop, upside down.

The roar of the engine was deafening, the sound vibrating in my ears. I saw my life literally flash before my eyes—moments racing past me, but in a strange, surreal way—everything seemed to go in super slow motion, yet fast at the same time.

It's hard put into words. But amidst the chaos, I also felt an overwhelming sense of peace, like a protective presence was nearby, shielding me. It was as if there was an angel right there with me, keeping me alive, keeping me safe.

In a state of shock and disbelief that I was still conscious, I looked over at my mom. She was dangling from the ceiling, still strapped in her seatbelt. I looked around the car, panicking, searching for a way to get out.

The engine was still running, and I was terrified that it might explode.

The car was smashed like a pancake, and I started banging on the window and the windshield, desperate to escape. Driven mostly by adrenaline, I grabbed the window handle and struggled to roll it up. Remember, we were upside down.

I unbuckled my mom's seatbelt, and together, we crawled through the narrowly opened window, just enough to slip out and escape the wreckage.

After getting out of the car, everything felt disorienting. I began screaming for help, blood gushing down my legs, broken glass embedded deep in my skin. Thankfully, despite the pain I wouldn't feel until later, I was standing. Alive.

A car came speeding toward us from the other direction, and a man and woman jumped out. They rushed over, asked if we were okay, and helped us into their car. This was before cell phones existed, and for some reason, instead of taking us to the hospital, my mom had them drive us home first, just a few miles away.

After getting us home, they finally managed to get her to take us to the hospital for examination and treatment. Turns out, I had a severe concussion, needed stitches in my knee, and had tons of embedded glass removed from my legs.

I was lucky to be alive, considering I could have easily been ejected from the car without a seatbelt.

My father was called, and he made the long drive from work to the hospital, which was at least an hour and a half away. I remember wanting someone—anyone—to help me. I was terrified of what had just happened but was afraid to say anything.

My mom, alone with me in the hospital room, confessed that she had wanted to die at that moment in the car, but remembered I was with her, and by that time, it was too late to stop the accident.

When my dad finally arrived, I felt a sense of relief wash over me. I knew I needed to tell him what had happened. My dad is an eternal optimist, someone who always looks for the good in everyone and everything—traits I'd like to think I inherited from him. But in that moment, I needed him to hear me.

When he asked what happened, I tried to explain as gently as I knew how. He couldn't believe what I described and thought I must be mistaken. He loved my mom so much, and I think he was unwilling to accept that she needed help. Instead of getting her the help she needed, he denied that anything was wrong.

Sadly, that day cemented a powerful yet hard lesson in my mind that I wish I hadn't learned: if I needed help, I would have to rely on myself.

For years, I developed a deep fear of trusting others. This fear became something I carried with me, making it hard for me to rely on anyone but myself. Keeping people at an arm's length felt safer than risking being exposed—or worse, let down.

That mindset kept me going for a while. It served me well in some ways, but it wasn't always the healthiest approach. And it's not sustainable. Over time, and with a lot of growth, faith, and counsel, I came to realize that seeking help from others—something I once resisted—was just as crucial for growth as trusting my own strength.

The Voice in Your Head

The car accident was just one piece of a larger puzzle that shaped my childhood. As you might imagine, the voices that echoed through our home weren't always kind.

"Are you stupid?" "How could you be so dumb?" "Don't touch that!" "Don't do that!" "Leave that alone!" These phrases became the soundtrack of my childhood, creating an internal dialogue that would take years to overcome.

How we talk to ourselves has everything to do with what we achieve, but much of our self-talk stems from the words we heard as kids. It's no wonder I became an expert in saying, "I'm sorry" and "I'll try harder." Those words felt like armor I could put on to protect myself.

Most days, I would retreat to my room, finding comfort in the solitude. It became my safe place where I could escape from the chaos. As the peacekeeper in our home, I didn't want to stir up any trouble. I just wanted to protect everyone, even the person who was supposed to protect us—the mom who, despite her struggles, tried her best.

It was a complicated dynamic, one where I knew my mom loved us, but at times, her high expectations and short patience made it hard to feel understood.

Looking back, I can see she was doing the best she could with what she had. She always made sure we had what we needed—food on the table, clothes on our backs, and a clean home. She worked hard and provided for us in every material way. I never doubted that she loved us. But emotionally, it seemed like she was carrying more than any one person should, and sometimes that pain spilled out in ways that left us all hurting.

Her mood could shift quickly, and not always in ways that were easy to predict. I often found myself trying to avoid any triggers and walking on eggshells, thinking that if I stayed out of the way, maybe things would calm down.

There were times when stress boiled over, and in those moments, things weren't always handled with patience and grace. I learned to anticipate what would happen, trying my best to stay out of harm's way. Most often, it was my brother and sister who bore the brunt of her anger, although I felt the emotional weight of it too. No matter what, I loved her, and I always found myself protecting her, even when I felt hurt or confused.

Now that I'm a mom—and a Mimi—I have so much more compassion for what she was going through and the internal battles she must have been facing. But I also believe it's important to get vulnerable and let others see beyond the highlight reel, which is why I'm sharing these memories with you.

One day, I remember a visit from Child Protective Services (CPS) during an elementary school Valentine's party. It's strange how clearly I remember the man's face. His eyes—cold, yet somehow searching—stayed with me long after.

When he asked me, "When did the lickings start?" my heart stopped. I had no idea what he meant. The word "licking" was foreign to me. I'd never heard of it before. His question was sharp, direct, and made me feel like I was about to be exposed for something I couldn't understand.

A sick feeling twisted in the pit of my stomach, and my throat tightened. I could feel the weight of his gaze, almost like he was waiting for me to say something, but I didn't know what to say. Was he accusing me? Was he looking for a confession I wasn't ready to give?

I stared back at him, frozen in that moment, but I denied any abuse. My voice caught in my throat as I instinctively protected my mom, even though I didn't quite comprehend what was happening.

Later, when I got home, I saw CPS at the house, questioning her. My heart sank, and I felt a mix of confusion and dread. But in that moment, I sensed that my mother's struggles came from a place of deep hurt rather than malice. My instinct was to protect her, even when I needed protection myself. That's the complexity of family love. We can be both wounded and healing, hurting and caring.

I didn't want to see her get in trouble, so I lied. I made up stories to shield her from whatever was happening. I couldn't make sense of it all, but I didn't want her to be blamed.

I remember feeling utterly lost, unsure of how to navigate this adult world, which was so confusing and overwhelming. I was just a kid, after all, yet somehow, I felt like I had to take on this responsibility that no child should have to carry.

That day, I was torn between the child I was supposed to be and the protector I had become. I was trying to shield my mom from the very thing that was supposed to protect us.

Even though I was hurting too, I stayed silent. I denied what was happening because deep down, I just didn't want to see her hurt, no matter how much it cost me.

I think this is where my drive to overachieve began—always trying to prove my worth. I spent many of my younger years trying to fit in and seeking approval, whether from friends or, you guessed it: boys.

Things at home were tough, and I longed for approval and acceptance. At 17, I found out I was pregnant, and shortly after, at 18, I got married. It felt like I was jumping from the frying pan into the fire—an overwhelming sense of uncertainty clouded my every step.

I was suddenly a young mother, navigating a new world with fear, self-doubt, and excitement all at once, which I didn't know how to process.

Rewriting Your Story

But here's where the story takes a turn. I had every reason to feel sorry for myself, to make excuses, and to give up. The voice in my head often whispered, "You're too young for this." "You're not prepared." "You'll never be able to make it."

Those negative thoughts could have easily consumed me, but through God's love and protection, He gave me the strength and ability to persevere.

As the years passed, what started as a difficult, overwhelming challenge slowly unfolded into the most beautiful journey of my life. My daughter became my greatest gift.

Instead of listening to the voice that told me I wasn't enough, I started to focus on the love and purpose that motherhood brought into my life. I realized that the story I was telling myself about being unworthy, scared, and incapable wasn't true.

I was stronger than I knew and capable of creating a life filled with love and joy, no matter how imperfect or uncertain the journey seemed.

This journey of self-discovery, healing, and love became the foundation I could build on, not only for my daughter but also for my three future daughters. The voice I had once heard telling me I wasn't good enough was replaced by the voice of love, resilience, and faith that encouraged me to keep going.

Every challenge, every sleepless night, every struggle with self-doubt—it all became part of a bigger story, one where I was the hero, not the victim.

Looking back, I see that the story I told myself when I was pregnant at 17 could have kept me stuck in fear and self-pity. But instead, I rewrote that story—one of strength, love, and growth.

The beautiful truth is that by changing the narrative I told myself, I was able to give all of my daughters a different kind of legacy. One that's grounded in love, resilience, and the belief that we can overcome anything by changing the story we tell ourselves.

Every stage of our lives molds us into the person we become, and I had a choice to make. I chose to turn pain into purpose. Was it easy? *NO.* Did I battle anxiety and depression? *Yes.* Did I always want to do the hard things to better my situation? *Absolutely not.* Did I overcome it and do it anyway? *You bet!*

At 18, I came to know Jesus as my personal savior, and over time, I discovered that my worth wasn't in anything other than Him, which was a huge relief. This knowledge gave me permission to be me. I didn't need approval or acceptance from anyone to know that I was worthy.

This was a pivotal time in my life, and I could finally heal and continue to grow into the woman that God called me to be. This isn't something that happens overnight; it's a process. One of the things I learned was that I needed a tribe of supportive and encouraging people around me, and I found that through church family, and crazy enough, direct sales.

Don't get me wrong—I was still choosy about *who* I allowed to speak into my life. But I learned to put myself in the space of people who were where I wanted to be—those who had the experience and wisdom to guide me. I learned that I needed to take advice from those whose lives reflected the success and values I aspired to, especially in business and personal growth.

I became grounded and rooted in my faith, and I stopped letting what other people thought affect me. I straightened my thinking through positive books, attending conferences, and seeing myself through the eyes of Jesus. I became laser-focused on my calling, and I got to work.

I knew deep within me that I was wired to win.

Where We Are Today

The stories I've shared represent some of our family's most difficult seasons, but they don't represent the end of our story. Healing is possible. Growth is possible. Transformation is possible—for individuals, for relationships, and for families.

Looking back with adult eyes, I can see how much my mother must have been struggling internally. A woman who would react out of anger was someone drowning in her own pain.

I also realize that back then, resources weren't as readily available as they are today. I don't remember having a single conversation during my childhood about brain health or personality disorders. It wasn't like we could look up symptoms on the internet or turn to social media to find out we weren't alone. We've come a long way, and help is a lot more readily available.

I have done significant work to heal from my past and break generational cycles. My relationship with my mom today looks vastly different from those painful early years. It's been built on mutual understanding, forgiveness, and the recognition that we were both doing the best we could with the tools we had at the time.

I've learned that hurt people hurt people, but healed people heal people. My mother's love was always there, even when it was expressed through the filter of her pain and struggles.

Today, she is one of my greatest supporters and champions, and I am grateful for the woman she has become and continues to become.

The courage to face our past, seek help, and choose healing over hurt has transformed not just individual lives but the trajectory of our entire family line. The legacy my daughters are inheriting looks radically different from the one I received, not because we pretended the past didn't happen, but because we chose to let it teach us rather than define us.

This is why I believe so deeply in the power of community, counseling, faith, and the willingness to be vulnerable. None of us has to remain trapped by our worst moments or our most painful seasons. We all can grow, heal, and become the people we were meant to be.

If you see yourself in any part of my story—whether as the child who endured trauma or the parent struggling under overwhelming pressure—please know that your story can change too. It's never too late to seek help, extend grace, or begin again.

Key Takeaways to WIN

- **You don't have to do everything alone.** Learning to trust others and ask for help can make your journey easier and more rewarding.

- **You can choose to be the hero of your story**. The past doesn't define you—the story you tell yourself shapes your future. You have the power to transform your self-talk and overcome any limiting beliefs.

- **Hurt people hurt people, but healed people heal people.** The person who caused you pain may have been drowning in their own struggles. While forgiveness doesn't excuse harmful behavior, it does free you to move forward.

- **It's never too late to begin again.** Resources and support are more available now than ever before. Remember, grace and second chances can redefine any relationship or life trajectory.

- **You are worthy of success, just as you are.** Embrace who you are and don't let fear or past experiences hold you back from achieving your dreams.

I Dare You to Take Action

I dare you to reclaim your power.

You've seen how the words we hear as kids can shape our self-talk and influence our choices. But your past doesn't get to decide your future. It's time to rewrite the story and step into your power.

Ask yourself:

- What limiting beliefs from my past are still holding me back?
- How can I change the story I tell myself?
- What can I do today to believe in my worth and purpose?

Once you've identified those old stories, challenge them. Notice the patterns of doubt or fear, then shift your focus to your strengths, resilience, and your faith.

Here's your challenge:

Choose one area where self-doubt has limited you and replace it with a belief that empowers you. Affirm your worth, reconnect with your purpose, or take one brave step forward even if fear shows up.

Success doesn't come from comparison—it comes from owning your story and growing from it. Reclaim your power. Rewrite the narrative, believe in yourself, and step into the future you were created for.

FROM ROCK BOTTOM
TO REDEMPTION

The truth is, I shouldn't be where I am today. If you lined up the facts—if you saw all the trauma, the brokenness, the mess—I might be the last person you'd expect to be writing this book, sharing a message of purpose and possibility. But maybe that's exactly why I am.

After the accident, my life took a sharp turn. On the outside, I was still that straight-A student, the one teachers believed in and friends looked up to. But on the inside, I was unraveling.

I didn't know who I was anymore. Everything became about proving I was enough. Seeking approval. Trying to fill a void I didn't yet have the words for.

In the middle of that identity crisis came something no 12-year-old should ever endure—sexual abuse. A 16-year-old boy that I had a crush on took advantage of me. Because I cared about him and didn't want him to get in trouble, I never told an adult about it. I would rather protect someone else than protect myself.

I was a child, and I wasn't capable of understanding the weight of that moment or the way it would shape me. Looking back, I realize that my virginity wasn't something I gave freely—it was something that was taken.

Although, at the time, I thought it was my fault. That's what abuse does—it twists things. It convinces you to silence your voice out of fear, loyalty, or shame.

That experience shattered something inside me. It marked the beginning of years spent chasing validation in all the wrong places. My teen years became a blur of partying, promiscuity, and pain, even recklessly experimenting with drugs a few times, trying to numb what I didn't know how to heal.

The summer I was 16, I moved out to live with some friends at the beach. I thought I was free—even if just for a few months. But it wasn't long before I wound up in a relationship that looked like love but felt like control. He was charming until he wasn't. Then the threats began: "If you ever leave me, I'll kill you—and myself." I didn't know if he was serious or not, but I was young, scared, and completely unprepared for the chaos that followed.

I used to wonder if it even counted as abuse. He never actually hit me. But he shoved me hard into a wall once, threatened to kill me or himself if I left, and controlled me with fear. Now I know abuse doesn't always leave bruises. Sometimes, it just leaves you afraid, confused, and convinced it's your fault.

At the end of that summer, I left and went back home. By October, I found myself right back there again—clinging to the hope that somehow, I could make it work. Because sometimes, broken love still feels better than being alone.

That was the night everything came crashing down. I was drinking and smoking pot. It was laced with something, and I overdosed. Someone called 9-1-1 and I was taken to the hospital in an ambulance. I had an out of body experience where I saw myself from outside of my body, surrounded by nothing but darkness.

I cried out to God, desperate, pleading for another chance. Some people said it was a hallucination. For me, it was a warning and a wake-up call. I knew if I had died that night, I wouldn't have gone to heaven. And that terrified me.

Weeks later, I found out I was pregnant. Unsurprisingly, he wanted nothing to do with the baby—and pressured me to have an abortion. That was the last time I ever saw him.

College-bound, top of my class, and now carrying a child I hadn't planned for … I was alone, scared, and ashamed. Depression and anxiety didn't just show up—they consumed me. The fear was constant. The shame was suffocating. I felt like I was drowning, and no one could see it.

At 20 weeks, I went into preterm labor and spent a few days in the hospital to stop it. I was put on meds and spent the rest of my senior year on bed rest, finishing school from home.

In the middle of all this, a longtime friend stepped in—someone I had known since I was 15. His name was Corbit. He loved me through my brokenness. We got engaged in the spring and married that summer. Most people didn't even know he wasn't the biological father of my daughter. But he was the one who showed up when it counted.

Still, by that October, I hit rock bottom again. Postpartum depression took over everything in me—my thoughts, my body, my days. I couldn't breathe under the weight of it all, and I had a tremendous fear of dying.

One morning, I felt this undeniable nudge to get in my car and drive to a little brick church I had passed a thousand times before. I didn't even know why—I just knew I needed something different.

At the end of the service, the pastor gave an altar call. I waited until everyone left, then approached him with trembling hands and a hundred questions. Most importantly: "How can I know I'm really saved?"

He smiled gently and said, "Susan, the Bible tells us that 'all have sinned and fall short of the glory of God' (Romans 3:23), but that 'God demonstrates His own love for us in this: While we were still sinners, Christ died for us' (Romans 5:8). Salvation isn't about what we've done—it's about what Jesus already did for us on the cross."

Then he shared these verses with me from Romans 10: "If you declare with your mouth, 'Jesus is Lord,' and believe in your heart that God raised Him from the dead, you will be saved."

Right there, with his invitation, I bowed my head and prayed—not just words, but a surrender. I believed. I confessed. I received the grace I didn't deserve.

And friend, maybe you're reading this and wondering the same thing: *"How can I know?"* The truth is, you can. If you've never made that decision, you can whisper it right where you are. Tell

Him you believe. Ask Him to forgive you, to come into your heart, and to make you new.

"Everyone who calls on the name of the Lord will be saved." Romans 10:13 (NLT)

He's not waiting for perfection—just your surrender. That same grace that met me on that day is available to you right now. That day, my life changed forever. I surrendered my heart to Jesus. And for me, it wasn't subtle. It felt like thunder and lightning— like the weight of my past collided with the grace of God in the most beautiful explosion of mercy.

From that moment on, I wanted to live every day with purpose. I knew I didn't go through all of that for nothing. The pain wasn't pointless. It was a setup. God didn't just rescue me—He repurposed me.

A few years later, I had a vision. I saw a sea of women gathered before me, and I was on a stage speaking to them, not from perfection, but from redemption. From restoration. From real, raw experience. That night, I knew without a doubt that my story would be my calling card. My pain would become the platform God would use to reach others.

And here's what I've come to believe with every fiber of my being:

If the enemy had his way, I'd be dead. Or lost. Or too buried in shame to ever rise. But God had another plan. He allowed every broken piece, not to destroy me, but to deliver me.

I shouldn't have been a success. But I am.

Not because I did everything right, but because I let Him make things right. What the enemy meant for harm, God repurposed for redemption.

Key Takeaways to WIN

- **Your past doesn't disqualify you; it prepares you.** Every painful moment can become part of your purpose when placed in God's hands.

- **God is not afraid of your mess.** He steps into it and brings meaning.

- **You can rise again.** No matter how far you've fallen, you are never too far gone for redemption.

- **Pain is often the birthplace of calling.** What you've survived might be exactly what someone else needs to hear to find hope.

I Dare You to Take Action

I dare you to look at the pieces of your past—not with shame, but with new eyes. What if the very thing you've been hiding is the thing God wants to use most?

Ask yourself:

- What painful parts of my story have I been afraid to share?

- Could my testimony be the key to someone else's breakthrough?

- What would it look like to fully embrace the fact that I've been rescued for a reason?

You are not disqualified. *You are called.*

Here's your challenge:

This week, write out your own redemption story. No filter, no edits—just you, the raw truth, and a God who never gave up on you. You don't have to share it yet. But write it. Read it. See the power in it.

And when you're ready, let it lead others to freedom.

YOU WERE MADE FOR MORE

At some point, someone may have told you to stay put. Play it safe. Stop dreaming so big.

"Be realistic."
"You're wasting your time."
"That's just a pipe dream."

But deep down, you know better. Those voices don't define you. You weren't made for small dreams or safe choices. You were made to break barriers, rise above expectations, and create a life on your own terms.

Imagine letting go of every *"should"* and *"don't"* that's ever held you back. Picture the freedom of chasing what truly sets your soul on fire. The thrill of stepping into the unknown, knowing you're exactly where you're meant to be.

Yes, it's scary. Growth always is. But when you dare to dream big, the world expands. Opportunities appear where there were once walls.

And trust me—I know this firsthand.

Fueled by Doubt, Driven to Win

Like many in direct sales, I had my fair share of naysayers when I started my journey. People rolled their eyes. Some called it a pyramid scheme. Or my personal favorite—*"When are you going to get a real job?"* For some people, that kind of doubt would be enough to make them quit.

But me? Oh no.

If anything, those comments fueled me even more. Even if, deep down, I battled with those words, there was no way I was going to let them see me sweat. I was going to prove them wrong. I was going to win.

You see, I've always been a *make a way, find a way* kind of girl. I march to the beat of my own drum. So I made a decision—I wasn't going to quit. I was going to become the best student I could be, put in the work, and make this thing happen!

I had plenty of reasons why it *shouldn't* have worked. I was young. I had no car. No money. No college degree. If you looked at my circumstances, success probably seemed impossible.

But I had two things that mattered more than anything:

1. A dream in my heart
2. The will to win

And that was enough.

When you make that decision—when you decide that your tomorrow is going to be better than your yesterday—*you can win too.*

Standing Out from the Crowd

If you're a believer, you might feel like you're supposed to blend in, keep your head down, and just do your thing quietly. After all, humility is important, right? But truth be told, blending in and staying hidden isn't what we're called to do. In Matthew 5:16 (NIV), it says, "... let your light shine before others, that they may see your good deeds and glorify your Father in heaven."

So, what does this mean for you and your journey? When your heart is aligned with God's purpose, when you're using your success and leadership to honor Him, it's not just okay to stand out—it's actually *good*! You don't have to hide your light under a basket or play small. God wants you to shine in your own unique way.

Scripture says:

> **"For you were once darkness, but now you are light in the Lord. Live as children of light."**
> Ephesians 5:8 (NIV)

When you shine, it points people back to Him.

Standing out isn't about seeking attention, it's about owning your space and using your voice to inspire others. When you lead with honesty, integrity, and authenticity, you empower others to do the same.

And, truthfully, it's not about drawing attention to yourself—it's about drawing attention to Him. When you step into your calling, embrace your success, and shine in your God-given purpose, it's all for His glory.

Standing out doesn't mean being prideful or arrogant; it means being unapologetically authentic and bold, showing up as the person God made you to be, and using your talents, your story, and your leadership to make a difference. That's what can truly change the world.

I can't tell you how many times I was tempted to hide behind that paint van and avoid the spotlight. But every time I showed up, even with imperfections, it reminded me of how far I had come—and the story I was living was worth sharing.

It was more than just the car or the rank I was working for. It was about embracing the journey and trusting that every step was part of the bigger picture.

Don't Shrink Yourself—The World Needs Your Boldness

Looking back, I realize one of the biggest lessons I learned was this:

Don't shrink yourself to make others comfortable.

I could have played small. I could have let doubt win. I could have squeezed myself into someone else's mold, trying to fit their version of success.

But that's not what we're here to do.

Your dreams aren't meant to be limited. They're meant to stretch as far as your mind can reach.

So, if you have a dream—whatever it is—pursue it. Don't let outside voices drown it out. Stepping into the unknown is uncomfortable. But there's power in discomfort. That's where transformation happens.

Forget the rules. Stop worrying about what others think. The world doesn't need you to play small—it needs you to show up, fully and unapologetically.

People Are Watching—Even When You Don't Realize It

One of the most surprising things I learned along the way was that my worst critics eventually became some of my biggest cheerleaders.

The same people who once doubted me, who rolled their eyes or whispered behind my back, were suddenly reaching out, asking how I did it, telling me they were proud, and even asking for advice on how they could start something of their own.

At first, I didn't realize they were paying attention. But they were. People are *always* watching, even when you don't think they are.

Some are watching, waiting for you to fail. Some are watching, curious to see if you're serious. And some are watching because, deep down, they're hoping you prove them wrong— not because they want you to fail, but because they need to see *someone like them* succeed first before they can believe it's possible for themselves.

You never know who you're inspiring just by showing up and refusing to quit.

The Decision That Shapes Your Future

When you make the decision that you are *going to win*—not *try*, not *hope*, but truly commit—you change the game.

You stop letting other people's opinions dictate your actions. You stop waiting for permission. You stop letting fear keep you stuck.

The truth is, people will always have something to say. Some will doubt you. Some won't understand your vision. Some will project their fears onto you.

But *they* don't have to live with the regret of you not chasing your dream. *You* do.

Dream big. Dream bold. Take the first step toward the life you were always meant to create.

Momentum, One Win at a Time

The best way to make progress? Break your big goals into smaller, manageable steps.

When you focus on the next right move instead of the entire mountain ahead, things feel less overwhelming. Each small win adds up. Each step builds confidence. And before you know it, you're rolling with momentum.

Let's not forget—failure isn't the end of the world. It's just part of the process. Every successful person has tripped, stumbled, and made mistakes along the way. The difference is, they didn't let those moments stop them.

Instead of letting failure knock you down, see it as a lesson. What can you learn? How can you adjust? How can you use this as fuel to keep going?

Bringing It Full Circle

The biggest breakthroughs in life come from *decisions*. Not over-thinking. Not waiting for the perfect moment. Just deciding.

I look back now at that girl who started with no car, no money, no degree—just a dream and the will to win—and I smile. Because I know what she didn't yet understand:

That all the doubt, the obstacles, and even the criticism were part of the journey.

That the people who laughed in the beginning would later ask how they could do it too.

That the very thing I was once unsure about would become the thing that eventually gave me freedom, confidence, and a life I once only dreamed of.

And if that girl could do it? *You* can, too.

Make the choice. Take the step.

And just watch what happens.

Because your next big win is just **one decision away.**

Your story is still being written. Your dream is still waiting for you.

You weren't born to fit in. You were born to stand out. **You were born to WIN!**

Key Takeaways to WIN

- **Facing fears helps you grow.** Pushing past fear is where confidence is built. Don't let it hold you back.

- **Other people's opinions don't define your future.** You are the only one who gets to decide how far you go.

- **Small wins lead to big success.** Take one step at a time, celebrate progress, and build momentum.

I Dare You to Take Action

I dare you to step up.

You've learned the power of boldness and what happens when you push past fear. Now it's time to act. I dare you to stop shrinking yourself and start embracing the big dream inside you.

Ask yourself:

- What thoughts are telling me to hold back?
- What dreams have I ignored because of fear or doubt?
- What bold decision have I been avoiding that could move me closer to my goal?

Once you see where you've been playing small, take one step toward that dream. Maybe it's reaching out to a potential customer, posting something vulnerable, or finally moving forward on the idea you've been sitting on.

Here's your challenge:

Take one bold step this week—no matter how scary. Message one person, make one call, or share one honest post about your journey.

Momentum grows through action, and each step pulls you closer to the life you're meant to create. The only thing standing between you and your breakthrough is a decision.

Dream big, take the step, and show yourself that you were made for more.

AFTERWORD

$\mathcal{S}$tanding at the edge of a new chapter in my life, I felt a mix of excitement and uncertainty. After spending 30 years in Direct Sales—18 of those as a Top 1% leader—I decided to take a leap of faith into something new.

I wasn't sure what would happen or who would walk that path with me, but deep down, there was a quiet voice telling me it was time. And sometimes, that little voice knows exactly what we need.

Looking back now, I'm overwhelmed by the outpouring of love and support I've received since making that leap. It's been a powerful reminder that when we trust ourselves, incredible things can happen.

One of the greatest gifts of this new chapter has been the chance to pour into other female entrepreneurs—not just as a mentor, but as someone who continues to chase her dreams, unapologetically. No longer do I have to choose between my personal ambitions and supporting others; I've found a way to do both, and that has been deeply fulfilling.

Through it all, I've learned that magic happens when you align your passion with your profession. When you're brave enough to follow your gut—even when the outcome is unclear—you open yourself up to a life far greater than you imagined.

To the women out there who are standing on the edge of a new adventure: I see you. I know how scary it can be. But I also know how rewarding it is when you trust yourself, take the leap, and step into the life you were meant for.

Create the Life of Your Dreams

I could have just daydreamed about the moment when everything would finally fall into place, hoping for the opportunity that would magically appear—the perfect break that would catapult us into the life of our dreams.

I could have told myself, *If I'm patient enough, if I work hard enough, if I just wait long enough … it will come.*

But the reality is, it's not coming. Not like that. The life you want—the one you keep imagining—isn't something that happens *to* you. It's something you *create.* And the sooner you realize that, the sooner you can start building it.

Think back to when you were a kid. You didn't sit around waiting for someone to hand you a plan. You just *created.* Whether it was building sandcastles, making up games, or turning cardboard boxes into rocket ships, you didn't wait for permission. You simply *began.*

That same creativity, that same instinct to dream and build, still lives inside you. It's just been buried under years of waiting, doubting, and hoping someone else would open the door for you. But no one is coming to do that. If you want it—really want it—you've got to get up, go after it, and build it yourself.

And here's the hard truth: it won't be easy. You'll stumble. You'll face setbacks. You'll have days where you wonder if you're crazy for even trying. But *every step* you take, even the difficult ones, is shaping you into the person who can handle the dream you're chasing.

Because the greatest stories? They're never about the people who sat back and waited for something to happen. They're about the ones who *created* their own opportunities—the ones who dared to bet on themselves, even when it was hard.

So here's my challenge to you: *stop waiting*. Stop hoping the "perfect moment" will come. It won't. Instead, grab what you have—the dream in your heart, the passion in your gut, the vision in your mind—and start. Right now. Right where you are. With what you have.

Because the greatest risk isn't failing. *It's never trying at all.*

Women Wired to WIN

The life you want is on the other side of action. So go. Build the dream. Take the risk. Bet on yourself. And when you look back, you'll realize the magic wasn't in the opportunity that came to you—it was in the moment you decided to *create* it.

But you don't have to do it alone.

If you're ready to take that leap—to stop waiting and start *winning*—I'd love to personally invite you to join our community of like-minded women who are *wired to win*.

Inside **Women Wired to Win**, you'll find support, inspiration, and practical tools to help you turn your dream into a reality.

Because the journey is always better—and more powerful—when you're surrounded by women who *get it*.

Join us here:

community.womenwiredtowin.com

Your time is now. **Go get it!** I'll be cheering you on every step of the way.

ALL OF YOUR LINKS IN ONE PLACE

You'll find each of these links throughout the book,
but I wanted you to have them all in one place
for easy access:

resources.susannormanonline.com

Your DISC Guide: How to quickly understand and connect
with anyone to book, sell, and recruit more!

discguide.susannormanonline.com

Your Swipe Files with 40 "Because" Power Statements to
unlock the words that move people to buy, book, and join—
without being pushy.

because.susannormanonline.com

Book, Sell, and Recruit like a Rock Star with
these magic scripts!

rockstar.susannormanonline.com

A powerful strategy to easily book appointments from leads to boost your results and do it BIG!

21daybooking.susannormanonline.com

Recruit with confidence using this 40-page guide. It's a great resource to use with your team.

shesaidyes.susannormanonline.com

Create videos that connect with your audience and build a brand that people remember.

makeitreel.susannormanonline.com

Never worry about what to post with this 365-Day Social Media Content Calendar. With a whole year of post ideas and prompts, you can show up, shine, and grow your biz without the stress of wondering what to say.

contentcalendar.susannormanonline.com

BONUS

Your Top 10 Systems for Success

Here are the top 10 systems that I've used to make all this possible, in one place:

1. **Social Media to Grow Your Brand**

   Remember: You are the brand, NOT your company. Build a professional page or business profile to attract people by showing them what you bring to the table. This is how you create trust. Once you have their trust, invite them to take the next step—join your Facebook group or subscribe to your email list.

2. **Onboarding Systems**

   Your new team members need guidance. Set them up for success with:

   - A welcome video
   - Training on the basics
   - Tips for booking appointments and managing their time

3. **Team Apps and Platforms**

   Use apps like Linktree or Milkshake to give your team a one-stop place for all the resources they need.

Simple, efficient, and easy to use. Example of my former team app:

teamhub.susannormanonline.com

4. Email Capture and Automations

Capture potential clients' emails using forms. Whether it's for a free event or a promotion, use automations to follow up, convert, and keep the conversation going. Watch my free training here:

landingpage.susannormanonline.com

5. Team Group Facebook Page

Use your group to keep everyone connected. Celebrate, recognize achievements, and track team goals. Host weekly events like Monday Night Live, Friday Focus, and career path events. Consistency is key!

6. Client ATM Group (Add, Tag, Message)

Create a team FB group where you can add, tag (in a welcome video), and message prospects. This is a great way to showcase your product or business opportunity before they buy or join. Be intentional with how you welcome and engage with new members.

7. Text and Email Campaigns

Automation is your best friend. Use platforms like Skippio or Project Broadcast to set up text campaigns. These systems help generate sales, recruit new team members, and book appointments on autopilot.

8. Content Creation Tools

Create engaging, short-form videos with tools like iMovie, CapCut, Filmora, or even Instagram Reels. For eye-catching graphics, use Canva to make your content stand out.

9. Scripts for Success

Don't reinvent the wheel. Use proven scripts, like the 21-day booking system, to stay consistent in following up with leads. Automate this process with text platforms to save time. Adjust as needed for your industry:

21daybooking.susannormanonline.com

10. Recruiting Funnel

Tired of chasing down recruits? A recruiting funnel can help you attract the right people without the hustle. A well-built funnel saves you time, attracts quality leads, and grows your team faster. See example of one of mine here:

info.themakeupmimi.com

Learn how to build your first recruiting funnel here:

recruitingfunnel.susannormanonline.com

ACKNOWLEDGMENTS

To everyone who has supported me on this journey—whether you walked beside me, cheered from afar, or simply believed in me—thank you. You've made this chapter richer than I ever dreamed possible, and for that, I am forever grateful.

To my Lord and Savior, **Jesus**, without whom nothing would be possible—Your grace, Your strength, and Your guidance are the foundation of every step I've taken. It is only through You that I've found the courage to dream big and the perseverance to keep going. So, for that, all glory and honor go to You first.

To my husband, **Corbit**, my ride or die—thank you for standing beside me through every high and low. Our journey has not always been easy, but it's been filled with love, laughter, and endless support. Through every challenge, you've been my rock, my partner in every sense of the word. This book, this journey—it's as much yours as it is mine.

To my beautiful daughters, **Kaela, Autumn, Amber, and Kara**—my "little women"—who have been my greatest gifts and biggest joys in this life. You've taught me more than I could ever hope to teach you. Your love, your light, and your unwavering belief in me have stretched me to grow in ways I never thought possible.

You've inspired me to be the best version of myself every single day. Watching you grow into strong, beautiful women fills my heart with so much pride. Every step of this journey has been for you, and I'll continue to push forward with the hope that I'm setting an example you can follow, just as you've done for me.

I am blessed beyond measure to have the love of you all surrounding me. My heart overflows with gratitude for the family who lifts me up every day.

I want to express my deepest gratitude to my coach and mentor, **Michelle Cunningham**. Michelle, you believed in me when I didn't even believe in myself. You saw potential in me long before I recognized it, and your unwavering faith in my abilities gave me the courage to push through my doubts and keep going.

Your leadership and guidance have shaped me in ways that I never could have imagined. You didn't just help me dream bigger—you helped me take the necessary steps to actually make those dreams a reality. Your wisdom, encouragement, and tough love have been invaluable, and I will forever be grateful for everything you've taught me.

This book, the success I've achieved, and the person I've become are all a reflection of your impact on my life. You inspired me to step outside of my comfort zone and show up as the best version of myself, even on the toughest days. I'm incredibly blessed to have had you by my side through this journey. Thank you for being a guiding light.

To my dear mentor and friend, **Tammy West-Murrian**, thank you for taking me under your wing all those years ago in my direct sales journey. Your belief in me during times when I doubted myself gave me the strength to push forward. You always saw more in me than I could see in myself, and for that, I am forever grateful.

Your encouragement, wisdom, and support helped me overcome many obstacles along the way. You didn't just show me the ropes—you helped me grow into the person I am today, both as an entrepreneur and as an individual.

Thank you for being not only a mentor but a true friend and leader in my life. Your impact will always be a part of my journey, and I will never forget the role you played in helping me become who I am.

Without **Lori Lynn,** none of this would have been possible. She didn't just edit my words—she dissected them, picked them apart, stripped them down, and then pushed me to go even deeper and find my voice as an author. Every step of the way, she challenged me to dig further, to uncover the heart of my story, and to be more honest and vulnerable than I ever thought possible.

Her relentless attention to detail and her unwavering belief in this book helped shape it into something far beyond what I imagined when I first began this journey. I am beyond thankful for her dedication, patience, and guidance. Because of her, this book turned out to be something truly special—and I'm amazed at what we created together.

Thank you, Lori, for making this book more than just words on a page. You brought my vision to life, and for that, I will always be grateful.

To **Shanda Trofe** and the incredible team at Transcendent Publishing: Thank you for bringing this dream to life with such artistry and excellence. From the perfect cover design to the stunning interior layout and thoughtful marketing plan, every detail exceeded what I could have ever imagined.

Your patience, guidance, and willingness to explain even the smallest details—again and again until I understood—made this journey not just smoother but deeply meaningful. You have a gift for making authors feel seen, supported, and confident through what can often feel like an overwhelming process.

Without your expertise and steady direction, I might still be stuck in the swirl of decisions. Instead, you and your team turned the final stage of this process into something beautiful, joyful, and seamless. I'm forever grateful for your professionalism, creativity, and the heart you put into every step.

To my incredible beta readers—especially **Susan Davis, Gwen Hardy, Dr. Darnyelle Jervey-Harmon, Jennifer Desrochers, Kim Logan, Lisa Taylor, Heather Brayshaw, Pam Vanderbilt, Lowell and Karen Martin, Kaela Revell, Alli Adkins, Katie Miller, Amy Campos, Kim Sailor, and Maggie Newhouse**—and my proofreading team, **Mary Rembert** and **Carli Odom**:

You held my words before they were polished. You gave your time, your eyes, your honest feedback, and your encouragement when I needed it most. Every note you sent, every suggestion you offered, every moment you spent reading this manuscript helped shape these pages into something better than I could have created on my own.

From the bottom of my heart, thank you. This book carries a piece of you in it, and I'll never forget the generosity and care you poured into this journey with me.

Finally, to the countless **friends, mentors, and fellow dreamers** who have poured into my life—though your names may not be listed here, please know that you are etched in my heart. Your support, your wisdom, and your belief in me have shaped this journey in ways I could never repay. You have all played an irreplaceable role in helping me get to this point. Shout out to some of you now.

ABOUT THE AUTHOR

SUSAN NORMAN helps direct sellers and network marketers **Dream, Plan, and WIN BIG** in their businesses.

Applying her 32 years of experience, Susan guides her clients toward creating a life of freedom with practical strategies that are easy to learn and implement.

In recent years, Susan has generated millions in personal sales revenue as an independent coach and consultant, specializing in high-ticket sales.

She has been recognized with multiple industry awards through the years, including honors as Top in Personal Sales, Recruiting, and Team Sales.

As the host of the *Women Wired to Win* podcast and the creator of the **Women Wired to Win** Facebook group, Susan has built a thriving community where women in business can learn, grow, and thrive together.

Susan and her husband, Corbit, have been married for an incredible 33 years. Together, they have raised four amazing daughters—Kaela, Autumn, Amber, and Kara—all of whom are happily married. And now Susan and Corbit are the proud grandparents of six beautiful grandchildren. They live in Smyrna, Delaware.

Her greatest joys are spending time with her family and inspiring others to stay true to their values as they chase their dreams.

To find out more and connect with Susan, visit:

SusanNormanOnline.com

YOUR FREE GIFT

First, thank you. Thank you for showing up for yourself, for leaning in, and for finishing this book. That alone proves you're wired to win.

As a way of celebrating you, I've created a special free gift: a **content calendar** to help you map out your game plan for winning in your direct sales business. It's practical, powerful, and designed to make your next steps easier.

This resource may not always be available, so grab it now while it's waiting for you. Plus, when you download it, you'll also get access to future resources I'll be creating just for the *Women Wired to Win* community.

thankyou.susannormanonline.com

I can't wait to see all the ways you'll put this into action. Remember—you're not walking this path alone. Your sisters and I are here, cheering you on every step of the way.

You've dreamed, you've planned …
Now it's time to WIN BIG!